DEMCO

A Young Woman's Guide to Health and Well-Being

The Tai Chi

Handbook

A Young Woman's Guide to Health and Well-Being

The Tai Chi Handbook

Ray Pawlett

ROSEN
PUBLISHING®

New York

This edition published in 2010 by:

The Rosen Publishing Group, Inc.
29 East 21st Street
New York, NY 10010

Library of Congress Cataloging-in-Publication Data

Pawlett, Raymond.
The tai chi handbook / Ray Pawlett.
 p. cm.—(A young woman's guide to health and well-being)
Includes bibliographical references and index.
ISBN-13: 978-1-4358-5360-7 (library binding)
1. Tai chi for women—Handbooks, manuals, etc. I. Title.
GV504.6.W66P39 2009
613.7'148—dc22

2009010316

Manufactured in China

Copyright © 2004 D&S Books Ltd.

Contents

Introduction

During the past few decades, the art of tai chi has spread out of China. The style has not been limited to a select few: millions of people worldwide practice tai chi. Part of the reason for this diverse appeal is the wide scope of the art. Indeed, if you try to define what tai chi actually is, you will arrive at a personal definition that may well differ from that of someone else.

It is with this in mind that I have written *The Tai Chi Handbook*. Its intention is to offer the reader insights across the scope of tai chi rather than information on one single aspect of it. Although my main background is in the Yang school of tai chi and five-element shiatsu, I have also studied many other styles of martial art, both "internal" and "external," healing arts, along with Taoist arts and meditation, too.

The exercises and examples in this book are written in a way that will enable you to try them for yourself. Always be sensible, however: if you know, or suspect, that a certain movement may cause you trouble, just skip it until you can ask a professional practitioner of tai chi for advice about it. Be careful with the applications as well, and remember that they are real. If you are training with a partner, be respectful of him or her and do your best to avoid causing injury. Note that the healing practices described in this book are not intended as a substitute for professional medical care.

What Is Tai Chi?

Tai chi is an ancient Chinese martial art system that is practiced throughout the world by ever-increasing numbers of highly enthusiastic beginners and veterans of the art. The vast scope of tai chi means that it is enjoyed by many cultures, young and old, fit and not so fit.

If you try to summarize tai chi, a basic definition is that it is a combination of a martial art, a healing art, and a philosophy. Each of these aspects is emphasized in different proportions by each of the millions of tai chi practitioners.

It can be said that tai chi itself is evolving. From the "old days" of tai chi, there are stories of students being badly injured in classes or having to hold a fixed position for hours on end. This type of training would be unrealistic for most modern people and times, and techniques are much changed. Nowadays, learning tai chi is a more refined and pleasurable process!

So what are the common aspects of tai chi practice? What will you get from your training, and what do you need to put into it? If this book can help you to answer those two questions, or look at them in a different way, then you will have made steps in your tai chi progress.

The Tai Chi Class

All tai chi schools follow a different style. Just as dance varies from tango and foxtrot to ballet and jazz dance, so there are many diverse styles and variations encompassed by tai chi. The traditional styles will contain elements of the following: health, martial art, and meditation.

Health

Tai chi is founded in traditional Chinese healing, which uses the concept of chi to explain health and disease. Tai chi is said to be excellent for developing your chi, as well as having further health benefits—well documented in the world of science—such as posture correction and stress relief.

Martial Art

Tai chi as a martial art involves learning a pattern or "form." Each movement in the form has one or more martial applications, which are then developed through exercises, such as pushing hands or other training drills. Once you have mastered bare-hand techniques at a high enough level, you will get the chance to expand your repertoire by learning tai chi weapons.

Meditation

The martial art applications in tai chi work better if your body is relaxed because the chi can move more freely and your body will move more efficiently. Your tai chi teacher should be able to teach you some meditation practices that will help you to gain the inner control and relaxation that tai chi can offer.

Is It For Me, and What Do I Need?

During the years that I have taught tai chi, I have had students of all shapes and sizes. The most extreme cases that I can remember are a gentleman in his eighties who only had one eye and a very highly skilled tae kwon do expert. Obviously, they were both looking for different things from the class. The elderly gentleman was looking for some gentle exercise, and the martial arts expert wanted to experience the martial arts that he already knew from a different viewpoint.

If, like most people, you fall somewhere between the two extremes, there is unlikely to be a physical reason for you not trying tai chi. If you are unsure, it is best to ask your teacher or doctor whether tai chi practice is suitable for you.

A common image of tai chi for many Westerners is that of the elderly gentleman rather than the martial artist. It is worth remembering that much hard work is required to reach the lofty heights to which tai chi aspires, so there really should be something for everyone.

The equipment needed for tai chi is minimal. Most people (including Chinese masters) usually train wearing either shorts

Any clothing that allows movement is suitable for tai chi.

or tracksuit bottoms and a T-shirt. I like to wear martial arts training shoes because they do not have a built-up heel, which can affect your balance. However, many people wear normal sneakers or train barefoot.

One thing that you will need is money. The cost need not be high, but you cannot expect to go to a class and not pay the instructor. If you are unsure about value for money, try looking at what instruction in other martial arts costs and see if it compares well. If you cannot afford it, try speaking to the instructor. You may find that you have something to trade.

In the end, the final choice is up to the individual, but all instructors should be aware that if it were not worth the money, their students would stop coming.

The Health Benefits of Practicing Tai Chi

So what can you expect to gain from practicing tai chi? If you invest time, effort, and tuition fees in learning the art, then it is reasonable to expect some benefits. The most common expectation is that it will be useful for stress reduction, and tai chi is certainly good for this.

A normal stress reaction is to start breathing quickly and shallowly. This is your nervous system going into "fight or flight" mode. While "fight or flight" can be a good response, it is possible for such instincts to be triggered when it is not appropriate. This can cause stress to your system and, over time, may result in illness.

Tai chi can help you to turn tension into calmness.

The slow, regular, and deep breathing in tai chi and qi gong exercises can help break this cycle, thereby reducing stress. The breathing exercises can also be useful for those suffering from such problems as asthma.

After practicing tai chi for a while, people often say that they feel more "grounded," and that they can cope better with the chaos of the world. One explanation for this is that the exercises in tai chi have opened up energy "meridians" that travel up and down the body. When under pressure, we can "ground" the energy, rather like a lightning conductor on a tall building. Without this grounding, it can feel as though energy is locked in the upper part of the body, trying to reach the earth.

Another significant health benefit of practicing tai chi is that it is very good for your posture, either in aiding the correction of an alignment that is already poor or in minimizing the effects of repetitive work, such as typing or using the telephone all day. Tai chi helps by keeping the spine and the muscles that support the spine strong and supple. This effect goes far beyond curing backache: if your body is aligned correctly, your internal organs will work

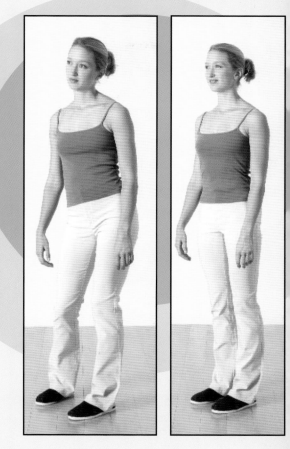

Tai chi gradually improves your posture.

efficiently and will not be compressed or stretched in unnatural ways.

The martial aspect of tai chi also helps your health because it "lifts the spirit." If you have strong spirit, you will become a more confident and happy person.

Internal and External Martial Arts

It is common to hear talk of "internal" and "external" styles of martial arts. If you were to ask the question "What is the difference?" the answer is likely to be vague, usually promoting whichever style that particular practitioner follows. However, in order to understand properly what the term "internal" means when applied to martial arts, it is a good idea to start with a little history.

The phrase first appeared in the year 1894. At the time, it was quite difficult to study more than one style of martial art, the reason being that, in those days, it was regarded as a challenge for a person from one school to approach another without provoking a fight! Eventually, it was agreed by three masters—Cheng Ting Hua, a ba gua zhang master; Liu De Guan, a tai chi master; and Liu Wei Xiang, a xing yi master—that it would be beneficial to all of their students if crosstraining were permitted between the styles. They had noted that the styles bore many similarities and that collaboration would be beneficial. The resulting martial arts "family" was given the name nei jia quan, or "internal family boxing," and the "internal" styles were born.

The aspects that the three styles had in common were primarily the use of "soft" techniques, chi development, circular techniques, and maintaining a relaxed mind rather than an aggressive attitude. Styles that employ these aspects as a part of today's training continue to be called "internal martial arts."

The main difference between internal and external styles seems to be in the approach to teaching. An external stylist, such as a karate or jujitsu practitioner, tends to learn the applications first, then becomes relaxed with the applications, thus developing more power, and finally seeks to increase that relaxation through such methods as meditation. The final result will always be similar, however.

The Roots of Tai Chi

Throughout Chinese history, warriors, poets, healers, sages, farmers, engineers, men, women, the old, the young, and just about any other types of people that you can think of have practiced tai chi.

Taoism

The roots of tai chi and many other martial arts reach into Taoism. To understand the history and techniques used in tai chi, it is therefore very useful to have a grasp of the basic concepts of Taoism. This will help you to understand the context within which the arts were devised, and is a way of learning about another culture and way of life that can enrich your own lifestyle.

Taoism is not a religion. It is certainly true that such concepts as the oneness of the universe are contemplated within Taoism, but no deity is worshiped and there is no belief in a supernatural power that governs the universe. This is not to deny such beliefs and concepts, however: Taoism can be "piggybacked" on a number of belief systems. For example, Mantak Chia, one of the foremost teachers of Taoism in modern times, is also a practicing Christian. His Taoism gives him a deep insight into his faith, which may have been difficult to achieve in more conventional ways. At the other end of the scale, many scientists have become interested in Taoism because its world view coincides in many ways with the discoveries of quantum physics and relativity.

Taoism derives from the observation of one's self in the universe and the interactions between the self and the universe. It is not as complicated as it sounds. For example, the seasons have an effect on us. When winter changes to spring, we feel changes inside ourselves. Without prejudging if it is good or bad, Taoists will notice these changes. Understanding your place in the world in which you live gives you the chance to feel a part of it.

There are various concepts, such as yin and yang and the "five-element theory," that provide the framework upon which Taoism is based. These concepts were also used in developing the martial arts, and are therefore worth looking at in greater detail.

The Taoist Idea of the Creation of the Universe

"It was from the nameless that Heaven and Earth sprang; The named is but the mother that reared the ten-thousand creatures"—excerpt from the *Tao Te Ching*.

A question that the Taoist sages contemplated was "Where did it all come from?" In their attempts to answer this fundamental question, the sages turned to the observation of the physical universe around them and meditation, through which the sages took themselves to a primal state of nothingness that they called "wu chi," or "the nameless."

In the original state of nothingness, Taoists believed that yin and yang—the two polarities in the universe—were equally matched and canceled each other out. However, the two opposites somehow came out of balance, causing perpetual motion, shifting from extreme yin to extreme yang, with moments of near balance somewhere in the middle.

As a result, the varying ratios and movements of yin and yang created all matter and energy within the universe. Such an image of creation has been represented in many ways, the most common of which in Taoism are the "five elements" (wu xing) and the "Book of Changes" (the I-Ching).

The five elements and the I-Ching can therefore be seen as representations of the universe, which was made by amalgamating the binary forces of yin and yang. These ideas may seem strange, but consider the ideas of modern physics for a moment. The most popular explanation in physics for the creation of the universe is the big bang theory. From the big bang, it is thought that the main elements, hydrogen and helium, were created. The hydrogen and helium then formed clouds that became stars. The "refuse" from these burned stars became the elements that make up the periodic table. When you consider that all atoms are made from positive and negative charges, it seems that the main differences between the ideas of the Taoists and those of the scientists is language.

Energy

In his famous $E = mc^2$ equation, Einstein proved that energy and matter are the same thing. This proof means that everything in the universe is made of energy. Here is another crossover between modern physics and Taoism. The Taoist perspective also states that everything in the universe is energy. This energy is called chi. Chi is a common concept in martial and healing arts. The words ki and prana, among others, are names given by different cultures to the same thing.

Chi is the name that is given to energy as a whole. Everything in the universe—a human, a piece of metal, or a plant—is made of matter and therefore possesses energy that the Chinese call chi. Nonphysical things, such as magnetic fields and radio waves, also have chi, the difference being that the chi is less dense (more yin). Living things have three sources of chi. These are the chi that you are born with, the chi that you get from your food, and the chi that you get from the air.

Two elements of chi are "jing" and "shen." For an entity to have life, it must have jing. Everything that is alive, whether plant or animal, has jing. For a living thing to have consciousness, it must have shen. In traditional theory, only humans have shen

Chi exists in everything, in different levels.

because it was thought that only humans have the power to know who, and what, they are. Yet tests by biologists have proven that many mammals, and possibly even some nonmammals, have a degree of consciousness, and in this context we could therefore say that there are varying degrees of shen.

Tai chi is said to be able to help you to regulate the usage of the chi that you were born with and to help you to use the chi from your food and breathing more efficiently. It can also increase one's self-awareness, or shen.

As consciousness evolves, a creature develops shen.

Meridians, Intent, and Tsubos

By now you should have a grasp of the concept of energy, or chi, and may realize that it has to move. Reduced movement of chi is the cause of illness in traditional Chinese medicine: if the chi moves, the body can be healthy; if it is restricted, the chi stagnates and illness can set in.

Imagine chi being like water. If you pump water through a pipe, it can flow. If you do not have a pipe, no matter how hard you pump, the water will not move very far. In chi, the pipe is the meridian and the pump is an internal organ, such as the liver or heart. There is a chi meridian associated with most of our vital organs. The organ for each meridian is the source of its chi. (But some organs, such as the brain, do not have a meridian associated with them.) Returning to the water analogy, if you want to pump water down a pipe, it has to go somewhere. You do not want to lose the water, but to keep it flowing, so you need a circuit. In order to make the system more efficient, and therefore last longer, you need a series of pumps along the circuit. This is exactly how the meridians are arranged. Organs are grouped together in pairs and the chi flows through those organs in a circuit. The aim of chi healing is to keep the chi moving freely within the circuit without too much leakage.

Chi flows freely like water when someone is healthy.

Most of the time, chi will flow within these meridian circuits quite adequately. Sometimes, however, a meridian pathway can become obstructed or weakened. If this were to happen in a water-pipe circuit, a way to clear the blockage would be to increase the pressure to force the blockage away. In such chi exercises as tai chi and qi gong, this increase in pressure is created through mind control. If you use your mind to "intend" the movement of chi, the pressure increases and the chi will move.

No pipework system would be designed without inspection covers, which can be removed for maintenance by an engineer.

In the chi system, these "inspection covers" are called "tsubos." Tsubos exist at various points along the meridians and are sometimes called "pressure points." A healer who uses chi can detect the location of these tsubos and will use his or her intent to move the chi along the pathway and clear a blockage. This is a fundamental way in which many chi healers work.

Energy meridians and tsubos are parts of the energetic body. If you were trying to find them by dissection, you would be disappointed: the only way to detect them is through using the sensitivity that can be learned as a skill.

Yin and Yang

As was already mentioned, in the Taoist vision of the universe there are two opposite entities called yin and yang, which are worth studying by the serious martial artist. The Chinese symbol for the yin-and-yang pair is the well-known tai chi symbol.

The Yin-Yang Symbol

The yin-yang symbol is a very clever piece of graphic design. Look at it for a while and think about what it may be telling you.

Start by looking at the colors, black and white. Black represents yin and white represents yang. The color black absorbs light, while the color white reflects light. In yin-and-yang theory, yin is the receptive, that is, it absorbs, and yang is the creative, which means that it expands. The reflective white light represents the expansion of yang and the contraction of yin is represented by the absorption of black.

So opposites can be described as being linked in pairs, for example, life–death, hot–cold, up–down, in–out, and so on, and this leads us to the idea that one cannot

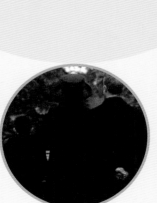

The opposites need each other in order to exist.

exist without the other.

The circular shape of the symbol suggests that the coexistence between the entities of yin and yang is cyclical. Yin must follow the extreme of yang, just as yang must follow the extreme of yin. A good example of this is breathing. After breathing in (yin), the energy becomes yang and you must breathe out.

Each half of the tai chi symbol contains a dot of the opposite color. This means that within yin there is yang, and within yang there is yin. One implication here is that yin and yang are not absolute, but are relative to one another: if I have a flashlight that is brighter than yours, it gives out more energy and is therefore more yang. If the sun comes out, it has much more energy than my flashlight, so my flashlight becomes yin, but it is still yang compared to your less bright one.

If you push your hand out for a strike, it is a yang movement because it is expanding, or moving away from, your body.

If you pull your hand back for a block or an interception, then the movement is coming toward you and is yin.

Punching is an outward, or yang, movement.

To repeat the movement, you have to pull your hand back before you can push it out again and vice versa. In yin and yang terms, you use yang energy when you push your fist out, but cannot do so again without pulling back and becoming more yin first. It would be like trying to breathe out twice in a row.

Roll-back comes in, toward your body, and is more yin.

Wu Xing—the Five Elements

Wu xing, or the "five elements" (sometimes referred to as the "five phases"), is a Taoist way of observing the world in which we live and our interactions with it. Records exist that show the theory of the five elements as having a history of around three thousand years: it is described in a book called the *Huangdi Neijing* that dates from the Zhou Dynasty, which started in 1122 BCE and lasted until 476 BCE.

The early Taoists would have derived much of their inspiration from observing the passing of the seasons and how they affect our physical and mental health. These observations became more sophisticated with the passage of time, and human physiological and psychological types were attributed to the five elements.

For example, if you are the type of person who loves the summer and hates the winter, this would be an indication that you are a "fire" type of person because summer is the time of year for the fire element. There are many subtleties and nuances to the theory, but this is the basic starting point. One of the uses of the five-element theory is to understand the needs of your body and mind throughout the passage of time and to be able to cater for those needs rather than

Sunbathing will appeal to fire energy.

either ignore them or respond to them in an unhealthy way.

Although few tai chi teachers attribute a certain move to a certain element, I have found the five elements very useful when teaching in helping me to identify the challenges that different people have in learning the movements. If you can identify an aspect of the tai chi form that is causing you difficulty, then you can use the five elements as a way of analyzing and categorizing that difficulty. This is a major step in solving the problem, and helps to harmonize chi flow through the elements.

Before describing the elements and how to apply them, it is worth pointing out that there are five of them and only four seasons. In Taoism, there is a fifth season: the transitional period between summer and fall, which is represented by the "earth" element. Some people call it an "Indian summer."

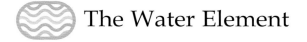 The Water Element

The water element is a good place to start because it is energy at rest, or energy in a state of quietness. The season for the water element is winter, when the world is frozen or locked into a dormant state. The energy that is locked into a seed is water energy, and you can imagine the seed lying frozen in the ground, waiting for the rising yang energy of springtime.

Water energy is the great void of emptiness that we enter during our sleep, and it is during deep sleep that our reserves of water energy are being replenished. The DNA contained within a seed before it grows is linked to water energy, which houses our "ancestral chi." This is like the information contained within the seed that tells the plant to be a sunflower instead of an apple tree.

Rest nourishes water energy. If you are not resting yourself, then your water energy

The coded information contained in a seed's DNA is water energy.

may become depleted. Meditation and good sleep (without the assistance of alcohol or other drugs) is beneficial. Drinking clean water can also help to maintain your water energy.

The organs for water energy are the bladder, which is a yang organ, and the kidneys, which are yin organs. The bladder meridian runs along either side of the spine and is particularly useful when treating back problems. If you are in water, the water will gently support your body. The bladder meridian works in the same way. The water energy in the bladder meridian supports your spine and helps to keep you upright. Posture is an important aspect of tai chi, and if you notice that your body slumps forward during your practice, it may be caused by the fact that your bladder meridian is not supporting your body.

Think a little deeper about water energy. Are you tired? Is your sleep disturbed or too short? A negative emotion for water energy is fear, so are you a fearful type of person? If this is starting to resonate with you, then you may need to consider the water element and how you can fortify it.

Rest and relaxation replenish water energy.

The Wood Element

After rest comes movement. Springtime is when water energy is transformed into wood energy. It causes seeds that have lain dormant in the soil throughout the winter to sprout saplings and the sap to rise in trees. On a beautiful spring morning, it seems as through nature is waking up after the darkness and long nights of the winter.

The time of day for wood energy is the early morning. Following the restfulness of sleep in the water-energy phase comes the waking of wood energy. Just as springtime

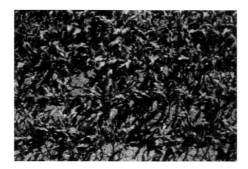

Wood energy creates growth.

leaps upon you in some years, while winter seems to drag on in others, we feel instantly alive on some mornings, but do not want to get up on others.

This brings us to another aspect of wood energy. If you are getting up to go on vacation somewhere exciting, it feels different from getting up to go to work. Two things may be happening here. The first is that if you are getting up for work, you do not have complete control over what you do. You have to submit an element of control to either your boss or your customer. The second is that you can use your imagination to "see into" the day. You know that if you are going to work, you will be there to work. If you are getting up to do your own thing, you will normally feel enthusiastic about it.

Vision and control are both aspects of wood energy. If somebody is exerting an influence that prevents you from seeing your visions through, this can lead to anger. Enough anger may lead to an explosion. Anger is a negative aspect of wood energy. An analogy for this is seeing weeds grow through the sidewalk. It may take many years, but eventually they will break through.

The organs for wood energy are the gall bladder for the yang half, and the liver for the yin half. The wood energy meridians control movement in the flanks of the body. This is especially true for the gall bladder meridian.

Working on tight deadlines can frustrate wood energy.

In tai chi, if turning the waist is a problem, think about the wood energy. Do you have an internal conflict in which you cannot decide which movement should be next? Can you "see" into the form so that you know where you are going with it?

Turning and decision-making are required in the form. If they are your weakness, think about your wood energy.

The Fire Element

The growth of springtime cannot last forever. If growth is unlimited, it cannot be sustained and will "burn out." After springtime, we therefore have the season of maximum yang energy: summer.

During this time, there is much activity in nature. Fruit swells and ripens on the trees. The migrating birds have arrived and are nesting. The leaves on the trees have grown and are absorbing energy from the sun. Nature is in its most active, or yang, phase.

Summer is the time when people get together and have garden parties, go to summer fairs, or simply relax. After the growth and vision of the wood energy in the springtime, there follows a need to express that energy. Without self-expression (fire), the power of the wood energy cannot be released, which means that the energy can become "stuck" in anger and frustration.

The time of day for fire energy is midday. This is an active period of the day, when we feel completely awake after the previous night's rest, but have not started to slow down and become tired, ready for the next period of sleep.

The organs of fire energy are the heart and small intestine. In Taoism, the heart is the center of love and happiness. When you

Creativity is linked to fire energy.

practice tai chi, do you have a passion for what you are doing, or are you just going through the motions? Can you express your inner self with the form? Are you actually enjoying it? If you are passionate about what you are doing, you must be enjoying it. This is an expression of fire energy within the form.

If you find that you are no longer in that state, maybe you need to look at different ways of expressing yourself within the form—release some of that fire energy! Remember that fire is the most active energy in the five-element cycle, which, if utilized, will allow you to take great steps forward.

 ## The Earth Element

Earth energy expresses itself at harvest time. This is the time when we gather in the crops so that we can feed ourselves. The nights are still quite long, but the crazy days of summer have passed, leaving a kind of grounded, warm, and mellow feeling.

The time of day for earth energy is mid- to late afternoon. It is a time when you have finished your midday meal and it would feel

great just to lie down in a hammock and rest for a while—if only!

The feeling of earth energy is one of "groundedness." It is the opposite of the head-in-the-clouds type of feeling that you

Harvest time is the season of earth energy.

Our feet and legs connect us to earth energy.

may experience if you live in your imagination. If your earth energy is healthy, there is a feeling of being in contact with your own body and with the planet Earth.

The organs of earth energy are the spleen and stomach. In energetic terms, they rule digestion, not just of food, but also of information and ideas. The creative aspect of fire is being assimilated into the body by the earth energy.

Earth energy has control over your muscles, especially those in your legs. In tai chi, we need strong legs. If this is your weakness, then the earth energy may need work. This will only come with regular practice to build up the muscles.

When you practice the form, it should be with your whole body and mind. If your body is doing one thing and your mind is jumping from one thing to the next, it is probably because you do not feel grounded. This means that you need to review your connection to the earth energy.

The Metal Element

As the year comes to a close and late summer turns to fall, the trees start to let go of their leaves, animals go into hibernation, and birds fly, or have flown, south for the winter. Nature is getting ready to hibernate, or to close down, for a while. The weather becomes cooler as yin starts to become stronger than yang. This is the time of year for metal energy.

It is the time when nature discards all that is not absolutely needed for the hibernation phase. It is the time of day when we relax and get ready for bed. We usually have some kind of ritual before going to sleep, whether it be

Grief is an expression of metal energy.

using the bathroom and putting on our bedclothes or saying a quick prayer before settling. These are all aspects of metal energy.

Another aspect of metal energy is division. Just as a knife cuts things into pieces, so metal energy cuts and divides things into smaller chunks. Metal energy can become lost in the past or in grieving for that which has gone. Just as death brings grief and memories of the past, the onset of fall and winter can bring sadness over the memory of the glorious days of summer.

The organs of metal energy are the lungs and large intestine. The lungs are the devices that give us chi from the air, while the large intestine eliminates waste. These functions both relate to our interface with the outside world. Metal energy is said to rule our boundaries. Skin is also ruled by metal energy.

Common challenges posed by the metal element are losing your breath during training, overanalyzing the form instead of just doing it, and worrying too much about the last mistake. Despite being a very challenging element, the clarity that it brings when you meet the challenge is undeniable.

Winter is the season for metal.

The Dance of the Elements

So far, the elements have been listed in the order in which they come into existence. This is known as the "creative cycle" of the elements, and can be summarized as follows:

- water gives life to wood by allowing the seed to germinate;
- wood can be used as fuel to create fire;
- fire creates ash that can fertilize the soil;
- earth, when condensed, becomes stone (metal);
- stones form the bed of a river and allow water to pass over them.

This cycle can be interpreted in many ways, for example, as the lifetime of a human, a day, a year, and so on. Another way of looking at the five elements, however, is in terms of a controlling or destructive cycle, as follows:

- wood covers earth;
- earth displaces water;
- water puts out fire;
- fire melts metal;
- metal cuts wood.

The two cycles can be combined to show the complete movements of the elements. An important implication here is that no element works in isolation, and that they are all dependent on one another to some extent.

Using the Cycles

By now, you know about tai chi and have contemplated the five elements. You may have identified a dominant aspect of the five elements within you that could do with some work, and may be ready to get started, but what now?

There are three straightforward ways in which you can use the five elements. Each will take a little thought and imagination to apply, but, with perseverance, results can be good.

1. Work on the Weak Element

The obvious solution is to work on the weak element. Meridian stretches and meditation on the element are straightforward ways of hitting the problem in this way. For example, if you decide that your water energy needs working on, try the stretch on page 66. It will loosen and gradually strengthen your back. Try imagining yourself floating in the sea—listen to music that helps you to relax. Think of your own associations with the water element and use them.

2. Use the Creative Cycle

There is a phrase in Chinese healing that can be roughly translated as "When the child screams, treat the mother." The logic here is that the energy from the creator (the mother) needs to express itself as the child. The mother will not be greedy and keep all of the energy, but will pass it on to the child in a way that can be accepted.

Returning to our example of the weak water element, think about why the element may be weak. It could be that you are just tired. It could follow that you are not sleeping properly because you are worried about things that have happened during the day.

If you can reinforce your metal element by having some kind of ritual that divides your sleeping time from your thinking time, you could get a better night's rest and thus pour strength into the water element.

Try different approaches to beat your tiredness.

3. Use the Controlling Cycle

Returning once more to the water element, it is possible that the level of the water has been raised by the addition of some earth. The earth element manifests itself in the muscles, among other things. This is especially true for the leg muscles because the classical meridians for the earth are in the legs.

If you can work on your leg muscles and make them stronger, they will support your body better and will assist the water element in its supporting role. This will usually be accompanied by a feeling of being more grounded, which will also help you to relax more.

These are just three of the many ways in which you could look at the five elements. For example, the water element could be weakened by the fire element or the wood element. Try to think of creative ways of using this tool for self-analysis.

Working the leg muscles can help the earth element.

The I-Ching

The five elements are just one of the Taoist methods of explaining the universe in which we live and our interactions with it. Just as there are no absolutes in yin and yang, so there are no absolute theories in Taoism, either. No single approach is described as "the one," and it is useful to have more than one way of observing the universe.

Another approach is that of the I-Ching, or "Book of Changes." Like the five elements, the I-Ching was used during the Zhou Dynasty around three thousand years ago. In excavations of a Zhou Dynasty site, turtle shells were found with markings that suggested that they had been used for I-Ching divination. It is known that turtle shells were used as money, but the markings suggest that the I-Ching was already well established by that time.

The theories of the I-Ching are connected with the Taoist idea of creation. From the original source, wu chi, come the two opposites, yin and yang, also known as tai chi. From the polarity of tai chi comes liang yi. This is a binary representation of yin and yang, with an unbroken line representing yang, and a broken line, yin.

Liang Yi

This kind of binary representation has resonance with modern computer technology. A binary word on a computer is made with binary digits, and the characters of the I-Ching are made in the same way.

—   **— —**

yang   yin

Si Xiang

By adding another line to liang yi, we derive four different possibilities or combinations. These four combinations are collectively called si xiang.

Ba Gua

The addition of another row gives us three lines, which are commonly called "trigrams," so giving eight possibilities, or eight characters, as shown on the next page. These eight characters are called ba gua in Chinese.

quian   dui   li   zhen   xun   kan   gen   ki

Each of these trigrams has its own name, such as ki, li, and kan, and each has been attributed different qualities, such as heaven, earth, thunder, and so on. The attributes are based on the balance of yin and yang within each trigram. These trigrams are the fundamental building blocks of the I-Ching.

In the I-Ching, greater subtlety and complexity are gained by linking two trigrams together. The trigrams are then grouped as an "upper" and a "lower" trigram, known as a hexagram. Grouping the trigrams like this gives sixty-four (8 x 8) different hexagrams in the I-Ching.

An interpretation of any hexagram is made by looking at the two trigrams from which it is created. The position of each trigram is important here: the lower trigram represents the internal, or hidden, part of a situation, while the upper trigram represents the external, or visible, part of a situation.

A central tenet of the I-Ching is that everything is in flux—all is changing, and nothing can stay the same. This is represented in a hexagram by having "old" and "young" lines, which are determined when the hexagram is cast, by using either sticks or coins.

An "old" line will change, that is, yin will become yang and vice versa. Therefore, if a hexagram is cast that has "old" lines, they will transform themselves into the opposite polarity, thereby giving a new hexagram.

The first hexagram, or the one that was cast, is said to represent the situation as it is, and the second hexagram—the one that has evolved—represents the situation as it may be.

The Meanings of the Trigrams

The I-Ching is regarded as a microcosmic view of the universe: an I-Ching casting is said to represent a snapshot of the energies within the universe and your relationship with those energies. The precise nature of a reading is guided by your intent. The idea is that the intent of your mind directs your chi. Your chi mingles with that of the world around you, and the hexagram gives a snapshot that represents the mix. The rest is down to interpretation.

While it is unnecessary to describe the meaning of each hexagram within this book, having an elementary understanding of the eight trigrams will give you an insight into the way that Taoist sages worked because the trigrams are the fundamental building blocks of the I-Ching.

Note that tai chi is a Taoist art, and that it can be said with certainty that many of the tai chi masters who developed the art used the I-Ching for inspiration. It is with this in mind that we discuss the I-Ching as a tool for exploring how we can improve ourselves by using tai chi, not as a tool for divination. Such notable thinkers as C.G. Jung used the I-Ching in this way.

The meanings of the individual trigrams are very deep and complex. They are deliberately symbolic, and the language of the I-Ching is always poetic. The following is a summary of what they mean.

1. Quian: the Creative

Quian is the most yang of the trigrams. The keyword is "strength." It is ruled by the principle of the father and its entity is heaven. The late fall to early winter is the time of year for quian.

2. Ki: the Receptive

Ki is the opposite of quian: it is the most yin of the trigrams. Its keyword is "devotion," and its family member is the mother. The entity for ki is the earth, and its time of year is late summer to early fall.

3. Zhen: the Arousing

Zhen combines the yang energy of the father with the
influence of the mother's yin and represents the eldest
son in the I-Ching family. His essence is in movement
and he is symbolized by thunder or wood. His time of
year is the springtime.

4. Kan: the Abysmal

Kan is the continuation of the effect of
the mother's yin upon the father's
yang, and his position in the I-Ching
family is the cunning middle son. He
is dangerous, although that danger may
be what is required to release a situation
from inertia. He is represented by water and
clouds. His time of year is winter.

5. Gen: Keeping Still

Gen is most influenced by yin energy, although that
of yang is still present. Gen is therefore said to be
the youngest son in the family. His essence is in the
stillness that is characterized by a mountain. His time
of year is late winter to early spring.

6. Xun: the Gentle

The yin lines now start to feature more, so the female principle dominates. Xun is the daughter most influenced by yang energy, so she is the eldest. Her nature is gentle and yielding, yet she has the power of penetration. Her manifestation is in the wind, and she shares wood with her elder brother. Her time of year is late spring to early summer.

7. Li: the Clinging

Li combines the yin and yang energies to become the beautiful middle daughter. Her nature is clinging, but she can be hot and agitated. Fire and lightning are her manifestations. Her high temperature gives her the summer as her season.

8. Dui: the Joyous

Dui is the yin element that is most influenced by yang. She is the youngest daughter; "pleasure" is her keyword and laughter is her voice. The lake represents her, and can be either deep or shallow, depending on the circumstances. Her time of year is the fall.

Using the Trigrams

These eight trigrams are built up to create the sixty-four hexagrams. When combined, their symbolic meanings give the full meaning of the hexagram. These hexagrams are very useful when searching for inspiration on a subject.

For example, hexagram number seventeen, called sui ("the following"), has dui, the youngest daughter, above zhen, the eldest son. The elder man is deferring control to the younger woman. This is the yielding concept in tai chi. By yielding to the lower position, the attacker's force is allowed to approach and is followed without resistance. This will give the advantage, because the force will be redirected and the defender will be able to control the next energy transformation.

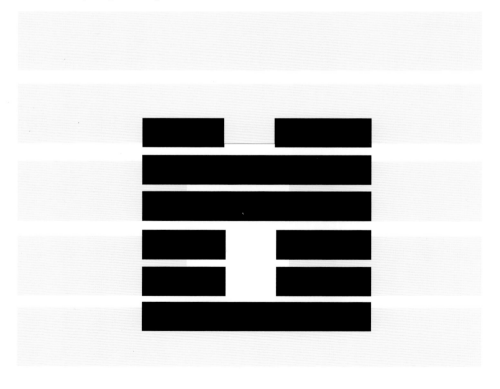

Wu Wei

Do you know the feeling of trying too hard? You are desperately putting every ounce of your being into getting something done, but seem to be going nowhere?

For me, it happens when I go ice-skating. I enjoy the pastime, but have no particular skill at it. I struggle to get across the ice, and if I am lucky, I do not fall over! If I am really in luck, I find my rhythm, only to see somebody float by me without seeming to move a muscle. The difference is that through practice, that person has learned to switch off the effort and simply skate, while I am still "trying" to skate.

This is what the Taoists call wu wei, the art of doing by not doing. It sounds impossibly contradictory, but then so do a lot of things in Taoism. It does not mean that things get done if you just leave them; it is about learning a skill to such a level that it becomes embedded. It may look and feel as though you are doing very little, but the actions you do make have the influence you want over the outcome that you desire.

In tai chi, we exercise wu wei. The beginner comes to the class and starts to learn the form. It is obvious, even to the uninitiated, that there is a difference between the beginner's form and the veteran's form. As with skating, the beginner is trying to do the form, while the veteran is doing the form. This is not to say that there is no effort in doing the form properly! It is about the fact that the conscious mind can let the subconscious do the work so that the form looks effortless.

Learn to flow with the movements.

The Middle Way

Chapter 9 of the *Tao Te Ching* says the following:

Stretch a bow to the
very full,
And you will wish
that you had stopped in time;
Temper a sword to its
very sharpest,
And you will find that it
soon grows dull.

Obviously, this is a fairly advanced stage. Here we are talking about the "middle way" that Lao Tsu wove into many of his chapters in the *Tao Te Ching*.

The idea is that yin and yang should be balanced. If you live your life in an extreme yang state, you will probably start by having a very exciting time. After a while, however, the excitement can either become meaningless or unsustainable.

Conversely, if you live in an extreme yin state, you could become so withdrawn that you no longer feel as though you are part of the world around you. Because much of Taoism is about integrating yourself into the world, this seems rather self-defeating.

Taoism teaches that the middle way is more sustainable and leads to a longer and happier life. This concept is embodied in tai chi practice. Even with the most yang of movements, there is a feeling of restraint— keeping within the frame of the movement. Without the restraint, it would be very difficult to make the transition back to a yin movement, so the tai chi would stop.

The Origins of Tai Chi Styles

Although there are many styles of tai chi, they are all based on five main styles. It is useful to know where your particular style fits into the world of tai chi.

2

Tai Chi Chuan: Historical Perspectives

When studying any art form, it is worth having at least a rudimentary understanding of its history. Such knowledge can lead to a deeper understanding of your art and how it has evolved through the years.

The history of tai chi chuan spans many generations, and its early origins have become clouded in legend. Different interpretations of its history abound. A common reason for this is that many of the schools like to see themselves as practicing the "original" tai chi because this helps to attract new students. Without doubt, a little romance has also been added to some of the stories to spice them up a bit. It may be that the true story of how tai chi really came into being is lost forever.

A common legend is that the immortal Taoist Zhang Sanfeng observed a bird trying to catch a snake. The snake was lithe and its movement soft. This made it impossible for the bird to catch it, so it escaped to wriggle around for another day. This is said to have inspired the movements that became tai chi chuan. The legend does have value because it emphasizes the idea of softness overcoming strength, which is a fundamental Taoist concept. It is still just a legend, however.

It is unconfirmed whether Zhang Sanfeng actually existed, although stories of his existence on the Wudang Mountain in China seem to have originated during the Ming Dynasty (1368–1664), probably at some point during the fifteenth century.

Fortunately, not all of tai chi's history is shrouded in vagueness. It is known that the Chen style of tai chi is the root of modern styles, and that all other styles derived from it or were highly influenced by it in some way. Most tai chi masters agree that there are five main styles of tai chi. These are Chen, Yang, Wu Yu Xian, Wu Jian, and Sun.

The Origins of Chen-style Tai Chi

Members of the Chen family were already known for their martial arts skills before they started to practice internal styles. They practiced a style called "cannon-pounding," or pao chui, which also involved elements of Shaolin red fist. The proximity of the Chen village to the Shaolin temple made this crossover of information straightforward.

The routines of pao chui, practiced by the Chen family, were integrated and simplified into two further routines, which became the Chen pao chui, primarily an external art, and were then developed into an internal art by Chen Wanting, although exactly how this came about is unclear.

The Chen-family lineage can be traced to the present day. A major influence was the advent of guns. Although the Chinese invented gunpowder, they did not invent guns. The scene on a Chinese battlefield would therefore be one of hand-held weapons and bare-handed combat until some time around the beginning of the twentieth century.

This had the same effect on tai chi as it was to have on many of the other martial arts, in that the battle techniques of each style took on a certain degree of redundancy. As a result, the styles evolved to include more of the spiritual aspects that had otherwise been associated with higher levels of the arts. Members of the Chen family travel the world today, bringing their very high level of skill to all who practice with them.

The Origins of Yang-style Tai Chi

The origins of Yang-style tai chi, although they may be slightly romanticized, are well documented. The first thing to understand is that the name "Yang style" does not have the same meaning as yang in yin and yang. It is a person's name, just as Chen is a family name.

The person that we are talking about is Yang Lu Chan (1799–1872). Yang Lu Chan was born in the village of Nan Guan in Yong Nian County in Hebei. His was a farming family. He was a very keen martial artist and learned a Shaolin style of kung fu in his early days.

Yang Lu Chan wanted to study the famous Chen-style martial art (it was Yang Lu Chan who popularized the name "tai chi"). In those days, things were different. You did not just find a club, turn up, pay your fees, and train. You needed to be accepted by the master. This was especially difficult with the old family styles unless you were a member of the family. This was not just being overprotective: they were trying to ensure that they could feed their families in the generations to come.

Yang Lu Chan, coming from a farming family, did not have the money to overcome this obstacle, but he did have the determination. According to legend, he managed to become a caretaker at the martial arts school in the Chen village. Through osmosis and covert watching of the training, he was able to gain enough information for his solo practice.

He was so determined that he reached a very high level of skill. A plausible story is that he was assisting a student of Chen Chang Xing. Chen Chang Xing had learned from Jiang Fa, so his skill was great. While unaware that the master was observing him, Yang Lu Chan taught the student to make some corrections.

Chen Chan Xing was so impressed by the humble caretaker that he tested Yang Lu Chan's skills. When he realized how serious the young man was about learning tai chi, he took him on as a student.

Yang Lu Chan went on to study the Chen style of tai chi for many years. He was never afraid to take on a challenge and became known as "Yang the invincible."

Yang Lu Chan had three sons, the eldest of whom died at a fairly young age. The two remaining sons were Yang Ban Hou and Yang Jian Hou. Both became skilled martial artists, although it is said that Yang Ban Hou had the most natural skill, and, by all accounts, a very bad temper. Yang Jian Hou in turn had a son named Yang Cheng Fu (1883–1936), who was to learn tai chi from his grandfather, father, and uncle. He was a very keen learner and his skill level became very high. It was Yang Cheng Fu who invented the Yang style of tai chi that is now the most popular in the world.

Yang Cheng Fu had two sons, who are still alive: Yang Zhen Ji (the eldest) and Yang Zhen Duo. Yang Zhen Duo has done much to popularize the Yang style of tai chi by traveling the world and teaching it to a high level. Yang Zhen Ji preferred to stay in his village in China and to develop his tai chi, making his form as close as possible to that of his father. He still teaches a small group of people, such as the tai chi master Christopher Pei, who has his own Wu Shu academy in Washington, D.C., and has a long-standing class with the Tai Chi Alliance, based in Nottingham, England.

The Origins of the Wu Yu Xian Style of Tai Chi

The founder of this style of tai chi was named Wu Yu Xian (1813–1880). Like Yang Lu Chan, the founder of the Yang style of tai chi, Wu Yu Xian was an inhabitant of Yong Nian County.

Also like Yang Lu Chan, he was a very keen martial artist with a background in Shaolin kung fu.

He and his brothers fell under the spell of the Yang family. Wu Yu Xian became one of Yang Lu Chan's students and assisted the master by teaching his sons to read and write. After a period of learning with Yang Lu Chan, Wu Yu Xian decided to try to learn from Yang Lu Chan's teacher, Chen Chang Xing. He was not able to learn from Chen Chang Xing, but was fortunate enough to learn from the famous Chen Quing Ping, who was also a very influential teacher in the Chen family.

Wu Yu Xian developed his own form, a mixture of those of Yang Lu Chan and Chen Quing Ping. The form uses small circles and a small frame. It is frequently practiced at different heights to emphasize different areas of development, such as strength in the legs or loosening the waist.

Wu Yu Xian did not have many students. One of his most skilled students was his nephew, Li I Yu (1832–1892). Li I Yu wrote *The Tai Chi Classics* and taught the art to Hao Wei Chen (1849–1920). Hao Wei Chen taught his style to Sun Lu Tang, who developed his own style of tai chi (see pages 48 to 49).

The Wu Yu Xian style of tai chi is one of the five major styles of tai chi, but is relatively unknown outside China. The Hao family descendants of Hao Wei Chen do much to publicize their art, and this style of tai chi is frequently called the Hao style in honor of their work.

The Origins of the Wu Jian Style of Tai Chi

Yang Lu Chan taught his tai chi at the Imperial Court of China, which was Manchurian. The fashion of the day was to wear long, flowing, silk robes. As anybody who has tried practicing martial arts can imagine, such robes make certain movements difficult to perform. Yang Lu Chan's answer was to create a Yang-style small frame for the Imperial Court. The small frame was essentially the old-style Yang form, but with smaller movements to accommodate the long garments that were part of the dress code of the time.

After the downfall of the dynasties during the beginning of the twentieth century, it was no longer safe in China to have a Manchurian name, so the family adopted the name Wu.

Wu Jian Quan and Yang Cheng Fu, the grandson of Yang Lu Chan, became practicing partners. Although the Wu Jian style of tai chi became separate from the Yang style of tai chi, the two families did not see them as being separate at that time.

It is said that Yang Cheng Fu would not allow rank or social position to alter how he trained with a person. When practicing push hands with a high-ranking official from a martial arts association, he did not hold back and "bounced" the person. Nursing his injured pride, the secretary general of the martial arts association decided to back Wu more than Yang, and thus the Wu Jian form split from the Yang form.

The Wu Jian style of tai chi is still popular throughout the world and has some very skilled masters. It is second only to the Yang style in worldwide popularity.

A Brief History of Sun-style Tai Chi

Sun-style tai chi is the most recently developed of the five styles. It was developed by Sun Lu Tang (1861–1933), a famous and highly skilled martial artist and intellectual of the time. Many legends exist about Sun Lu Tang, even though he died relatively recently. As is frequently the case, the real life of Sun Lu Tang sounds far more interesting than any of the legends.

Sun Lu Tang was born on January 4, 1861, in Wan County, near the city of Bao Ding in Hebei province. His original name was Fu Quan (the name Sun Lu Tang was given to him later by one of his teachers). Sun Lu Tang's father was a farmer. In the early days, Sun Lu Tang was not a physically strong boy, but his father recognized that he was very intelligent and sent him to a local scholar, who taught him reading and calligraphy.

At the time, the Qing Dynasty was in control of China and imposed heavy taxes that reduced the family to a state of poverty. When it raised taxes to an even higher level, Sun Lu Tang's father could no longer afford to educate his son. Shortly after the boy's studies ceased, Sun Lu Tang's father became ill and died. Sun Lu Tang's mother then managed to persuade a rich local landowner to take her son on as a servant.

At the time, Sun Lu Tang had found a martial arts instructor and was a keen and fast learner. Although his mother did not approve when she heard of his interest in martial arts, she agreed to let him continue his studies when she saw how much they had improved his fitness level. He was still employed by the landowner when, at the age of twelve, he was attacked by a martial artist eight years his senior. He hit the man in the stomach. This marked the end of his employment.

Sun Lu Tang then became the student of Li Kui Yuan, who taught him xing yi, or "five-element boxing." For the first year of his training, Sun Lu Tang was taught only the san ti posture. He became very skilled at xing yi, was accepted as a disciple of Li Kui Yuan, and wrote books on the subject.

Sun Lu Tang then met Cheng Ting Hua, a famous expert in ba gua zhang, another internal Chinese martial art. He was highly impressed by the evasive maneuvers used in the art and was accepted by Cheng Ting Hua as a student to learn the art. His studies made him very skilled.

In 1891, Sun Lu Tang took his teacher's advice and began to make a living by teaching martial arts. Again on the advice of his teacher, Cheng Ting Hua, Sun Lu Tang went to Wu Dang Mountain in Hubei province to study Taoism. On his return, he started a martial arts school in his town.

In 1914, Sun Lu Tang heard that the martial artist Hao Wei Chen was ill. He tended to Hao Wei Chen throughout his illness and became a friend. In return for his kindness, Hao Wei Chen taught Sun Lu Tang his style of tai chi, Wu Yu Xian.

Sun Lu Tang went on to integrate this tai chi with xing yi and ba gua. The result was the Sun style of tai chi. It is famous throughout the world and is less diluted than many styles of tai chi because Sun Lu Tang taught his daughter the style and she carried on teaching it after his death, thus ensuring that the style remains close to how her father would have wanted it to be.

The Chinese National Form

A popular version of tai chi is that of the Chinese national form. In 1956, the Maoist government released a book describing a form called "simplified tai chi chuan." It has twenty-four movements and is frequently called "the 24." The emphasis of the form is on the physical-health benefits that tai chi can bring. Because Taoism was not in favor at the time, the Taoist notions regarding the foundation of tai chi were not emphasized.

"The 24" was largely based on the Yang style of tai chi, although more demanding forms in terms of content and length were devised in consultation with masters from other styles. The resulting forms became known as the "combined forms," and were promoted by the Chinese government as a good exercise regime. Now very popular throughout the world, they have evolved slightly from the originals, and many teachers have integrated traditional Taoist and martial arts skills into them.

Tai Chi Practice: Getting Started

Tai chi warm-up exercises are vital to get the chi flowing through the body. The exercises should always help you to let go of tension.

3

Warm-up Exercises

In tai chi, the movements are usually performed at quite a slow speed. When an experienced person practices them, it can look graceful and effortless. In reality, however, the slow movements of the tai chi form are giving the body a workout that can be as strenuous as a session in the gym. Furthermore, the experienced tai chi practitioner will have her mind in a fixed state of calmness and heightened sensitivity, which allows the person to feel the chi within the movements. In effect, a mental workout is being performed at the same time as a physical workout.

Just as you would not weight-train without warming up, it is inadvisable to practice tai chi without doing so. It will prevent you from overstraining your muscles and will help to relax your mind and body before practicing the forms. The exercises shown here can either be applied to any other activity that requires physical effort or be used alone as a way of loosening up when you get up in the morning. You may find that you already know some of them.

I have given guidelines in the exercises as to how many repetitions to do. This is assuming that you are reasonably fit and have no problems that could hamper you. The person who ultimately decides how many exercises to do is you. If you want to do more or less, you can make the decision to do so. As with all of the exercises in this book, let your body be the boss. If you experience pain or discomfort from an exercise, either ease off or leave it out completely. If you are overenthusiastic and damage yourself, it will probably stop you from training for a few weeks. This is a distressing thought!

Neck Rotations

Most people know what it is like to have a stiff neck. A few simple neck and shoulder exercises can help prevent the problem. In tai chi, you need a strong, supple neck so that you can raise the crown of your head.

1. Stand in a relaxed position, with your head up, your shoulders down, and your feet slightly apart.

2. On an outward breath, let your chin drop down to your chest to stretch the back of your neck. Do not pull your head down, but let gravity do the work.

3. Hold for around 15 seconds if you are a beginner, and longer if it suits. Breathe in and lift your head up.

4. On an outward breath, open the side of your neck by letting your head fall to one side. Again, let gravity do the work. Do not pull it. Let your ear move toward your shoulder and do not lift your shoulder.

5. Breathe in and return to the center.

6. Repeat the side-pull for the opposite side.

Shoulder Rotations

If you become stressed, your shoulders can become hunched, causing painful knots in the muscles. The gentle use of these shoulder exercises can help to release the tension. In tai chi, the body must be loose, or "sung," as the Chinese say. If you start to relax your shoulders, the rest of your upper body will follow. Bear in mind that practicing the exercises slowly and controlling your breath is more effective than trying to do it quickly—it gives your body time to adjust.

1. Start in an easy standing position.

2. Breathe in and lift your shoulders as high as they will go.

3. Breathe out and rotate your shoulders backward, in time with your exhalation.

4. When you reach the bottom position, continue the circular movement of your shoulders as you lift them on the inhalation.

Repeat 8 to 10 times. Repeat the full movement, circling the shoulders in the opposite direction.

Shoulder and Elbow Rotations

This exercise is particularly effective for mobilizing the whole of the shoulder blades or scapulas. Next time you watch big cats on television, see how much power they generate from their scapulas. Loosening your scapulas allows you to do the same. Try not to hold the rest of your body rigid during this exercise, but let the movement flow through you.

1. Start in an easy standing position. Touch your inner shoulders with your fingers.

2. Breathe in and make a big upward circle with your elbows.

3. On the exhalation, pull your elbows down.

Repeat 8 to 10 times.

Windmill the Arms

When done slowly, this exercise will help you to loosen your shoulders. If you try doing it more vigorously, it will also work your cardiovascular system.

1. Start in an easy standing position. Put your fingertips into the soft part under your collarbone. (This will tell you whether you are lifting your shoulder instead of rotating it.)

2. Rotate your whole arm in one direction 10 to 20 times.

3. Repeat in the opposite direction.

Upper-body Twist

This exercise helps you to exercise the upper section of your spine.

2. On an exhalation, turn your body gently to one side.

3. Inhale and return to the center.

1. Start in an easy standing position. Raise your fists and elbows. Your fists should not be tightly clenched.

4. On the second exhalation, turn the same way, but a little farther.

5. Inhale and return to the center.

Repeat steps 4 and 5 on the opposite side.
Repeat the whole sequence 8 to 10 times.

Rotate the Waist

Waist rotations help you to exercise your lower back and loosen your waist. Your waist needs to be flexible to generate power in any martial art. For that reason, this exercise is practiced in nearly all of the martial arts that exist.

1. Start in an easy standing position. Place the palms of your hands on your kidneys.

2. Press forward with your hands so that your body arches forward slightly. Keep your head stationary.

After 8 to 10 of the large rotations, gradually reduce the size of the rotation until it stops. Repeat the exercise, rotating in the opposite direction. Try to make the same number of rotations in each direction.

3. Rotate your body in one direction, gradually allowing the size of the rotations to increase, but do not make the circles so large that your head moves.

Swinging the Arms

This exercise loosens your upper body and massages the ming-men and tan-tien points, both of which are considered vital for a healthy life by energy healers.

1. Start in an easy standing position.

2. Begin the exercise by rotating your waist backward and forward.

3. As the rotations increase in size, allow your arms to lift with the momentum of the rotation. Remember that your arms should be moved by your waist—do not swing them outward.

Repeat the rotations for a couple of minutes.
Then slow down and gradually stop.

Thigh Rotations

This exercise is especially good for developing the muscles that you will need for the kicks in the tai chi forms. It is also very good for your balance.

1. Start in an easy standing position.

2. Breathe in and lift up your knee in front of you.

3. Breathe out and bring your knee around in a circle as you exhale.

4. Repeat 3 to 5 times.

Change the direction of rotation.
Repeat for the opposite leg.

Knee Rotations

If done correctly, this exercise can help to prevent injuries to the knee, a common problem for athletes. If you already have knee problems, consult an expert before trying the exercise. If it makes your knees uncomfortable, skip the exercise.

1. Stand with your feet together.

2. Bend down and put your hands on your kneecaps (this helps to protect your knees). Focus your eyes on a spot on the floor (this helps you to balance).

3. Rotate your knees in a fairly small circle in one direction 6 to 10 times.

4. Repeat the rotations in the opposite direction.

Ankle Rotations

Ankle rotations help you to loosen the whole of your leg and keep your ankles supple for tai chi movements.

1. Start in an easy standing position. Shift all of your weight onto one leg.

2. Lift the heel of the other leg so that your toe is in contact with the floor.

3. Rotate your knee in one direction 8 to 10 times.

4. Keep your ankle soft, so that the rotations loosen it.

Repeat for the opposite leg.

Stretching Exercises

One of the aims of tai chi is to make the body soft and loose so that it can move lithely. If your body is supple, then it becomes resilient. It is like comparing a willow tree to an old oak tree. In a storm, the supple willow can flex more than the old oak tree, and so stands a better chance of weathering that storm.

By comparison, it should take little to understand the health benefits of keeping your body supple, and the only real way to make your body more flexible is by stretching your muscles.

Outlined in the following pages are six body stretches that concentrate on specific meridian pairs in your body, as detailed in the five-element theory (see pages 22 to 32). This means that you can supplement your mental grasp of the five elements with a physical understanding from performing the meridian stretches. Try to work out which is your best element for stretching and your weakest element for stretching. This can tell you much about your energy. Try using the creative and controlling cycles to give you a stretching sequence. Be creative—the tools are there for you to use.

Make sure that you are warmed up before stretching. This will enable you to perform a better stretch and will prevent injury. It is not a good idea to stretch when you have a full stomach because this can harm your body.

Try not to overdo a stretch. In some exercises, there is a "no pain, no gain" ethos, but not here! Instead of feeling the burn, savor the stretches and notice the different feelings that they give you.

The sequence of the meridians follows the "Chinese clock," which is based on the Taoist theory that some organs are more active at certain times of the day than others.

Stretch for Lung and Large Intestine Meridians

This stretch will work the meridians for the metal element. As with all of the meridian stretches, if you do not force them, but allow the force of gravity to do the work, you will actually feel the stretch along the meridians concerned. This stretch is particularly useful for opening the chest area. You may feel a little dizzy on completing this exercise. This is because your body has had a big burst of oxygen and it is now pumping around your head. Do not go straight into the next exercise, but allow yourself to regain your balance before moving on..

1. Stand with your feet slightly more than shoulder-width apart and your toes pointing slightly outward.

2. Link your thumbs behind your back. Spread out your fingers.

3. Take a deep breath.

Repeat, changing the grip with your thumbs.

4. On exhalation, release your body so that your torso drops forward in a controlled way (no sudden movements). Feel the maximum weight in the front of your feet. Breathe slowly and deeply.

5. When you have finished, inhale and push back with your hands to lift your torso. (If you think of pushing your hands back rather than lifting your body, you will avoid injuring yourself.)

Stretch for Spleen and Stomach Meridians

This stretch is for the earth element. It is particularly useful for the quadriceps at the front of your legs.

There are three different levels of difficulty with this stretch. Make sure that you are comfortable at one level before moving on to the next. If you try to force your body, you will not be able to feel the meridian being stretched and will lose your body alignment. The full stretch can sometimes pull the knee. If this happens, go back to an easier position to prevent it being damaged.

If you are comfortable with your weight on your elbows, lean back all the way, so that your back is lying on the floor. Intertwine your fingers above your head and breathe deeply. As you breathe in and out, feel the tension and relaxation in your muscles. Hold the position for a few breaths or for as long as you feel comfortable.

When you have finished, come out of the stretch in the same way that you went into it. If you made it all the way to the floor, support yourself on your elbows and then on your hands before returning to the kneeling position.

1. Start in a kneeling position.

2. Lean back and support your weight on your hands. (Most reasonably fit people will be able to do this.) Hold the position for a while and understand how your body feels. It could be that this stretch is deep enough for you. Move on only when your body is ready for more.

3. Increase the stretch by lowering your weight onto your elbows. At this point, you should be able to feel the stretch through your legs, and probably through the trunk of your body, too.

Stretch for Heart and Small Intestine Meridians

This stretch is for the fire element. It opens up the groin and loosens your upper back and neck.

1. Sit with your back held straight and the soles of your feet together. Hold your feet with your hands. As you inhale, bring your heels in, to your groin. If you cannot get your heels close to your groin, do not worry—the exercise has highlighted an area of stiffness for future work.

2. On an exhalation, let your torso drop forward. Release your neck and let gravity pull it down. If you can let your neck go, you will feel the stretch work through your back. If your neck is stiff, you will feel the stretch in your back less.

Hold the position for a few breaths and then come out of the stretch in the same way that you went into it.

Stretch for Kidney and Bladder Meridians

This stretch is for the water element. It stretches your hamstrings and also along your spine.

1. Sit on the floor, with your legs stretched out in front of you and your back held straight.

2. Take a deep breath and, on the exhalation, drop your body forward. If you can, grab your feet. Otherwise, hold your legs. Breathe into the stretch and let your neck relax so that your head drops down and stretches the upper part of your back.

Hold for a few breaths and stay relaxed. When you have had enough, inhale as you lift your body back up.

Stretch for Heart-Protector and Triple-heater

These meridians are from an elemental group called secondary fire. The heart protector is the pericardium that surrounds your heart and all other internal organs. The triple heater is not actually an organ: it is a regulation system for the organs. This exercise is good for opening the groin and the area between the scapulas.

1. Sit in a cross-legged position, but do not actually cross your feet over.

2. Pull your heels as close to your groin as you can.

3. Cross your arms over and hold your knees. If your left leg is in front of your right, your left arm should also be in front of the right.

4. On an exhalation, drop your body forward. You should feel the stretch in your groin and between your shoulders.

After a few breaths, come out of the stretch in the same way that you went into it.

Repeat, crossing your legs and arms the opposite way.

Stretch for Liver and Gall Bladder Meridians

This final stretch works with the wood energy. It is a very powerful exercise for opening the flanks of your body.

Meridians

1. Sit on the floor, with your legs wide apart. (The position of your legs should be comfortable because this stretch is not designed to open the groin area.) Keep your back straight.

2. Exhale, and stretch forward along one leg. You may be able to hold your big toe or ankle. If not, grab as far along your leg as you can.

3. Lift your other arm over your ear until it is pointing toward your foot. It is important not to twist your body because this will not allow you to stretch your flanks properly. Hold the position for a few breaths, then return to the center position.

Repeat the stretch on the opposite side.

Assisted Stretching

Just as many of the exercises in yoga are suitable for assisted stretching, or stretching in pairs, so, too, are the meridian exercises. For the tai chi student, or somebody who is learning healing work, this can be valuable practice for the person in the assisting role of the stretch because it helps you to learn sensitivity when working with a partner. The point of assisted stretching is not to try to reach a higher level, but rather to help the person being stretched to understand their limitations and keep their posture correct.

The feedback that a partner can give you is invaluable because it can help you to notice habits that have become so ingrained that you no longer notice that they are there.

In each exercise, the person who is performing the stretch is the active partner and the assistant, the passive partner. If you are the passive partner, work from a stable, well-grounded position. It is not going to help if you suddenly slip while assisting your partner; you may even cause injury if you fall on to her.

It is the responsibility of both partners to be sensitive to the limitations of the active partner.

Assisted Stretch for Metal

The active partner performs the stretch for the lung and large intestine meridians. The passive partner places one hand on the sacrum of the active partner and gently pushes the arms of the active partner with their forearm. This stretches deeper into the meridian. Be careful not to push too hard.

Assisted Stretch for Earth

The active partner performs the stretch for the spleen and stomach meridians while the passive partner gently pushes against the outside of the active partner's knees in order to encourage them to move closer together. (The stretch is most effective if the active partner can keep her knees fairly close together.)

Assisted Stretch for Fire

The active partner performs the stretch for the heart and small intestine meridians while the passive partner puts gentle pressure on the upper back of the active partner. Do not push too hard, but let the active partner find her limit and work with it.

Assisted Stretch for Water

The active partner performs the stretch for the kidney and bladder meridians, while the role of the passive partner is very similar to that in the fire stretch. Place one hand on the ming-men point between the kidneys and the other between the shoulders. Gentle pressure will allow the active partner to perform a deeper stretch.

Assisted Stretch for Wood

The difficulty with this exercise can be keeping the torso straight, allowing the stretch to work in the sides of the body. The role of the passive partner is to assist the stretch by keeping the active partner's body straight.

The active partner performs the stretch for the liver and gall bladder meridians while the passive partner places one hand near the hip and the other close to the shoulder and gives a slight twist, so stretching the active partner's outer flank. The stretch should be felt in the sides of the body.

Abdominal Breathing

In tai chi and qi gong, it is vital that your breathing supplies enough oxygen for each exercise. This is also true for stretching, where you need to learn to "breathe into" a stretch. There are many different breathing methods, the first of which is abdominal breathing.

One of the first things to learn is to be aware of how you are breathing. Sit upright and place your hands on your sternum in the middle of your chest. Feel the movement when you breathe in and out. Can you feel your lungs inflate as you breathe in and deflate as you exhale?

Now put your hands on your navel and repeat the exercise. Which had the most movement, your chest or your navel? If your chest was moving the most, your breathing is shallow—centered mainly in the lungs and upper chest—and prevents your lungs from working to their full capacity.

If your navel was moving the most, you are already doing abdominal breathing. This allows your diaphragm to work more efficiently and therefore draw more air into your lungs, thus increasing their capacity.

Furthermore, the gentle movement of the abdominal area helps to massage the internal organs and aids the peristaltic action of the large intestine. (Note the connection between the lungs and large intestine, both organs of the metal element.)

Place your hands back on your abdomen. Relax your body and blow the air out of your lungs. As you do so, push into your abdomen slightly with your hands. You will feel your hand move into your abdomen as you exhale. Now inhale and use the inhalation to push your hands away.

Standing Exercises

Much of the power in tai chi comes from the stance, or posture, that you use. The stances need to be strong, and in order to gain this strength, standing exercises are traditionally used.

Standing exercises work with the internal, core muscles—rather than the visible, external muscles—the muscles that help to support the body's weight. If you work out in a gym, it is possible that your external muscles are very toned and healthy, but your internal, core muscles may have been neglected unless your training specifically works on them.

There are accounts of tai chi students having to hold standing positions for hours before being accepted by a tai chi master. One thing that the master can be sure of in such instances is that the potential student has done some serious work to get to that stage. Standing exercises look very easy, but can feel difficult if you try to hold a position for a long period.

To benefit from standing exercises, you do not need to practice them for hours. Ten minutes a day can make a big difference. It all depends on what you are trying to gain from the exercises. When you start, you will probably find that five minutes seems like a lifetime. If so, gradually build up your time. There is nothing to be gained from rushing, but much to be gained from perseverance.

The standing postures that we will look at here are the wu chi position and the standing-like-a-tree position. The former is important because it is the starting posture for most tai chi forms and is the basis of all other postures. The latter is good for developing the strength in your legs and helps you to develop the ward-off technique (see page 121).

The Wu Chi Position

As an experiment, try standing in the wu chi position for twenty minutes. How did it feel? Did you last the twenty minutes? Could you keep your mind clear, or was it wandering?

The physical effort of standing in the wu chi position is not great. Most of us have stood for much longer while waiting in line or watching a band play. The difference with the wu chi position is that we try to switch off random thoughts in the mind, a process that is part of tai chi training.

When you can stand in the wu chi position for twenty minutes, try moving on to the more demanding, standing-like-a-tree position (see page 74).

Head upright, mind calm.
Soft focus in the eyes.
Neck relaxed.
Shoulders loose.
Back straight.

Arms loose.
Steady,
deep breathing.

Legs straight, without
locking the knees.
Feet parallel
and shoulder-width apart.

Standing Like a Tree

This standing position is popular throughout nearly all of the tai chi schools. There are many different versions, such as wider stances, different arm positions, and standing on one leg. The popularity of the exercise is a testament to its effectiveness. It has the advantage of needing very little space to practice it, so that it can be performed anywhere.

The starting position for the exercise is the wu chi position (page 73). If you have mastered the wu chi position to the level where you can hold it for about twenty minutes, it will help with this exercise. The standing-like-a-tree position is more difficult than the wu chi position and uses different muscles, so if you feel as though you are starting at the beginning again, do not worry. You are actually going up a level.

A more advanced way of practicing this exercise is to combine it with the microcosmic-orbit meditation (see pages 113 to 114).

Head upright, mind calm.
Soft focus in the eyes.
Neck relaxed.

Shoulders loose.

Back straight.

Arms curved, as though holding a large ball.
Armpits open.
Elbows relaxed.

Fingers pointing toward each other, with the thumbs held up.
Steady, deep breathing.
Slight tilt of the sacrum.

Knees slightly bent.
Legs straight, without locking the knees.
Feet parallel and shoulder-width apart.

Tai Chi Stances

In tai chi, the stances are designed to be as natural as possible. The idea is that if you train in a stance that already makes sense to your body, it will be easier for you to adopt and integrate the exercises into your life.

There are five main stances. They may vary from style to style, but the fundamental elements remain the same.

Wu Chi Position

This appears as the opening and closing moves when practicing the tai chi forms.

Horse-riding Stance (Right)

This is similar to the wu chi position, except that the knees are bent. Be careful to keep your back straight.

Head upright, mind calm.
Soft focus in the eyes.
Neck relaxed.

Shoulders loose.

Back straight.

Slight tilt of the sacrum.

Knees slightly bent.
Legs straight, without locking the knees.

Feet parallel and shoulder-width apart.

Bow Stance

The bow stance is among the most common stances used in tai chi. The power of the stance is in its forward movement. In empty-hand forms, the bow stance is used for most of the attacking postures, in which you move toward the person you are attacking.

If you have ever pushed an automobile or used a saw, you will most likely have already used a version of the bow stance. Try it out by standing up and pushing against a wall as hard as you can. Most people will adopt a bow stance for a push. In tai chi, we refine the bow stance to make it stable and adaptable to change.

There are variations of the bow stance that tend to center on the orientation of your back. In traditional Yang-style tai chi, for example, if you are pushing in one direction with your hands, your back will line up with your leg. If you are pushing in two directions, as in the single-whip movement, your energy is split, which means that your torso will be vertical.

Push Variation

Back straight.
Torso in line
with the back leg.

Eyes forward.
Shoulders down.
Elbows relaxed.
Wrists relaxed.

Back leg straight,
but not locked.

Sixty percent of your
weight on the front leg.
Forty percent of your weight
on the back leg.
Shin perpendicular
to the floor.

Stance is
one-and-a-half times
the width of your shoulders.
Front foot straight.
Back foot at 45 degrees.

Split Variation

Eyes forward.
Shoulders down.
Elbows relaxed.
Wrists relaxed.
Equal effort in
both directions.

Back straight.
Torso vertical.

Sixty percent of
your weight on the front leg.
Forty percent of your weight
on the back leg.
Shin perpendicular to the floor.
Back leg straight, but
not locked.

Stance is one-and-a-half times
the width of your shoulders.
Front foot straight.
Back foot at 45 degrees.

Getting Into the Bow Stance

1. Stand in the wu chi position (see page 73).

2. Slide one foot back, approximately one-and-a-half times the width of your shoulders.

3. Turn your right foot to an angle of 45 degrees.

4. For the push variation, push both hands forward as though you were pushing an automobile.

5. For the split variation, pull your hands apart as though you were opening a pair of sliding doors.

Drop Stance

The drop stance is only used for the low positions that are sometimes performed in tai chi. The stance is used for the movement snake creeps down. The most common fault when performing this stance is leaning forward with your body. This breaks tai chi principles because you lose your balance. The best way to stop this from happening is to try not to drop beyond your limit. If you go too low, you will lose control and lean. If you look at photographs of the Yang and Chen families, their drop stances do not lean forward.

Torso straight.
Back straight.

Sink onto the back leg.

Front foot flat on the floor.

Same foot position
as for the bow stance.

Empty Stance

In the empty stance, most of your weight is carried on your back leg. It is generally a defensive, or retreating, stance, but can be used for an attack, especially in the sword form. This is quite a demanding stance for the beginner because all of your weight is on one leg. Be careful not to rise up when your legs become tired because this lifts your center of gravity and makes you less stable. This stance is quite common throughout tai chi, and is used in such movements as hands strum the lute and repulse monkey.

Getting Into the Empty Stance

1. Stand with your heels touching each other at an angle of approximately 45 degrees.

2. Bend both knees slightly so that you can take your weight on your back leg.

3. Put one foot forward and settle down lower on your rear leg.

Head up.
Shoulders down.
Back straight.

Sink onto your legs.
All of your weight is on your rear leg.
The leading leg is "empty," or carrying no weight.
Knees bent.

Slight angle on the leading leg.

Tai Chi Walking

Tai chi walking can be regarded as a kind of meditation. When you practice tai chi walking, your attention is directed toward your feet. When you concentrate on your footwork, it is difficult to be in the kind of mental state when you keep going over things in your mind. In other words, you become more grounded.

In all tai chi stepping exercises, and in the tai chi forms, you should always aim to keep your body at the same height. You should not bounce up and down, but should sink your weight onto your legs. Grip the floor with your toes to increase your feeling of connection with the earth.

Tai Chi Forward Walking

1. Start in the bow stance, with your left leg forward.

2. Sit back onto your right leg. Allow the toes of your left foot to lift, but do not allow your left knee to lock.

3. Turn your body to an angle of 45 degrees to the left.

4. Shift all of your weight from your trailing right leg to your leading left leg.

5. Press your left leg into the floor, so that your right leg starts to feel lighter.

6. Step forward with your right leg into a bow stance. Your heel should touch the floor first.

7. Your heel is followed by the ball of your foot. Finally, grip the ground with your toes.

8. Sit back onto your left leg.

9. Turn your body 45 degrees to the right.

10. Shift your weight from your left leg to your right leg.

11. Push into the floor with your right leg and lift your left leg.

12. Step forward into the bow stance with your left leg, heel first.

13. Place your foot down and grip the ground with your toes.

Repeat until you get to the other side of the room.

Tai Chi Side Step

1. Start in the horse-riding stance (see page 75).

2. Sink all of your weight onto your left leg.

3. Release your right leg and move it to the right. Touch your toes down first.

4. Then touch down your heel.

In tai chi, the phrase "being double-weighted" means dividing your weight between your legs equally. It is a mistake in tai chi to be double-weighted. In the bow stance, for example, you have 60 percent of your weight on the front leg and 40 percent on the back leg. The side step fools many people because it looks as though you are double-weighted. The shifting of weight in this exercise is a little tricky for the beginner, but perseverance will get you there.

7. Touch down with your toe and then your heel. Shift all of your weight onto your left leg.

6. Lift your left leg and draw it toward you.

5. Move your full weight over, onto your right leg.

Repeat the steps.

Tai Chi Back Step

The most difficult aspects of going backward are balance and how far to step. They are actually linked. It will be difficult for you to balance if you try to step too far, so start with fairly small steps. It is better to have a short stride that is correct than a long, unbalanced one.

1. Start in the empty stance (page 79), with your weight on your right leg.

2. Sink your weight onto your right leg and allow the toes of your left foot to lift.

3. Step back with your left leg and put the ball of your foot on the floor.

4. Touch the floor with your left heel, with your foot at an angle. Your weight should still be on your right leg.

5. Twist your waist counter-clockwise and force your weight down onto your left leg. As your waist shifts your weight, allow the movement to straighten your right foot.

Repeat until you cross the room.

The Essence of Tai Chi

In tai chi, all movements have a meaning and specific body requirements. Understanding these meanings and requirements will enrich your practice.

4

Flowing-movement Exercises in Tai Chi

Most tai chi forms are fairly long and involve many intricate movements. Trying to learn everything in one go is a very difficult task. Think about a musician. When a musician learns a piece, he will not try to play the whole tune at once. He will look at the scales first and make sure that he knows them, then he will practice the individual phrases and, finally, he will put the whole thing together.

Tai chi uses similar logic. The tai chi equivalent of the scales are the flowing qi gong exercises. They give you the chance to teach your body the arm movements while in a static position. This allows you to concentrate on what you are doing with your upper body before looking at what you should be doing with your lower body.

The exercises have value in themselves. They will help you to move chi throughout your body, to work your muscles, and to strengthen your body. There are literally thousands of different qi gong exercises devised by different masters for different purposes. Here we will take a look at using movements from the qi gong exercises and then developing the exercises into tai chi movements by adding lower-body movements.

Waving Hands Like Clouds

For all of the exercises, try to direct the movement from your waist. Do not just wave your hands, but keep your body involved. Do not overexert your breathing: try to keep it natural. If it feels wrong at first, allow your body to make changes in its own time. Do not try to force anything.

Stage 1: One Hand

1. Start in the horse-riding stance.

2. Extend the fingers of your right hand, keeping them relaxed.

3. Inhale and raise your forearm to the level of your chin.

4. Continue the inhalation and extend your arm.

5. Exhale and press down with your hand. Do not try to press hard: go with the flow of the movement.

6. Begin the inhalation cycle when you have completed the press down with your hand.

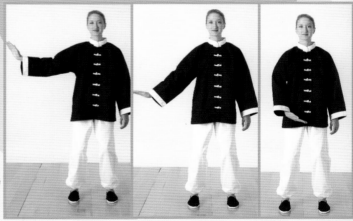

When you are proficient with your right hand, try the left.

Stage 2: Two Hands

Only try two hands when you have mastered the movement with both hands individually.

Repeat the movement in exactly the same way that you used for the individual hands, but with both hands instead. The difficult part is timing when moving two hands. If you ensure that the central position guards your throat and groin and your hands move in opposite directions in the extended position, you will be close to the correct movement.

1. Start with your right hand at neck level and your left hand in front of your tan tien.

2. Press down with your right hand and push upward with your left hand.

3. Your left hand should now be at neck level, with your right hand in front of your tan tien.

4. Press down with your left hand and push up with your right hand.

Stage 3: Stepping

The stepping movement for waving hands like clouds is the side step. You should step on the inhalation (yin movement) and press your hands together on the exhalation (yang movement). To perform a powerful yang movement, keep both feet on the floor, otherwise you will lose your balance.

Brush and Push

Start the exercise using one hand only. When you can perform the movement fluidly with your right hand, learn how to do the same with your left hand.

Stage 1: One Hand

1. Start in the horse-riding stance.

2. Inhale and circle your right palm outward to lift it to shoulder level.

3. Exhale and push your palm outward.

4. Start the inhalation (yin) cycle as soon as you have fully extended your arm.

Repeat the exercise.

Stage 2: Two Hands

When you can perform the movements for each individual hand smoothly, try using both hands together. When your right hand pushes outward, your left hand should push down and vice versa.

Stage 3: Stepping

The step for brush and push is to step forward in the bow stance. Your timing should be such that when you push, your back leg becomes straight. The nonpushing hand can be regarded as a blocking hand.

Strum the Lute

There is no stepping required for strum the lute, and the exercise makes better sense if both hands are used. The reason for this is that the movement is always executed with two hands in the forms.

Stage 1: In the Horse-riding Stance

The horse-riding stance makes the movement less demanding on your legs because it requires less strength. This enables you to concentrate on the movement of your hands.

1. Start in the horse-riding stance.

2. Extend your right arm forward.

3. Pull back with your right arm and simultaneously lift your left arm.

4. The yang part of the movement is when your right elbow pulls downward and the fingers of your left hand point upward.

Repeat the movements so that your hands are moving in vertical circles.

Stage 2: In the Empty Stance

In the tai chi forms, this movement is executed in the empty stance because it is primarily a defensive movement. Practicing in the empty stance is exactly the same as practicing in the horse-riding stance except that your standing position is different. Follow steps 2 to 4 on page 91 to execute the movement.

Keep your posture correct and the movement smooth. This will help you to build up the strength in your standing leg especially because it carries 100 percent of your weight.

Part the Wild Horse's Mane

To start with, try this as a single movement with one arm (we have not yet reached the stage where the movement becomes cyclical). When you can relax with the movement and can follow the shoulder, elbow, and hand sequence, try it with the other hand.

Stage 1: One Hand

1. Start in the horse-riding stance.

2. Turn your waist counter-clockwise and place your right hand, palm upward, just below your navel.

3. Turn your body, and, as you do so, use the movement to project your right arm forward. Think about moving in the sequence shoulder first, elbow second, and hand last. Keep the movement smooth and your body straight.

Stage 2: Two Hands

1.

2.

3.

1. Start in the horse-riding stance.

2. Turn your waist to the left and put your right hand below your navel, in the same way that you did for the single-hand exercise.

3. The difference for the two-handed exercise is that your left hand goes to a position above your right hand.

4. Turn your body and project your right arm forward in the same way. This time, as your right hand moves outward, press down with your left hand. The left hand becomes the reaction hand and gives more power to the movement.

5. Keep your body turning in a clockwise direction and repeat the exercise on the opposite side.

6. Use your left hand to project outward and your right hand as the reaction hand.

4.

5.

6.

You are now in a position where you can repeat the exercise in a cyclical way. In the first instance, many people feel the power in the movement and try to emphasize that aspect. If you go the other way and try to emphasize the softness, the exercise will train your body more efficiently and you will develop more power in the long run. Try to see how gently you can do the exercise. Keep your movements continuous and remember that you should exhale on the outward, yang movements. You will probably soon feel some interesting sensations that are caused by the movement of chi.

Stage 3: Stepping

The steps for parting the wild horse's mane are made in the bow stance. Follow the movements in the photographs. The timing should be that your weight sinks down onto your leading leg when your leading hand finishes its outward projection.

A Word on Intent

The phrase "an iron fist in a velvet glove" neatly describes an aspect of tai chi. The movements should look very soft and graceful, but should also have an innate power that flows with the movement.

Without this inherent strength, the tai chi exercises merely become an interesting series of callisthenics.

So how do we transform the movement? The answer is by using intent.

My engineering training gives me my own way of defining intent using an electrical circuit as an analogy. Electrical power is a product of current and voltage. In basic terms, current can be described as a flow of electrons and voltage as the force that makes the electrons flow.

Chi works in a similar way. Chi is the raw energy, like the current in an electrical circuit. The chi cannot flow without intent, just as the current cannot flow without voltage. Therefore, if the intent is absent, no chi will flow. Obviously, other analogies could also be used, such as water pressure in a pipe.

So what is intent and how do we use it?

As its name suggests, intent comes from the mind. The basic postulate is that you use your mind to move your intent and the chi will follow. This is bad news for those tai chi students who like to switch off during practice. It is true that you should try to switch off such thoughts as "I wonder what to have for dinner," but your mind should never be blank during the form.

The next exercise—unbreakable arm— and the grounding aspects that follow will teach you ways of putting intent and chi into your form.

Unbreakable-arm Exercise

This exercise is used to teach the difference between using your internal strength directed by your intent and using muscular force. It is a little bit like weight-lifting for your intent.

At first, the exercise may seem quite strange to you, especially if you know somebody who can already do it in a very powerful way. Do not try to be a super-woman. The type of person who is very good at the exercise will probably have practiced it already. If you tried to do the same as that person, it would be like walking into a gym and attempting to lift heavy weights on your very first visit.

The secret is to notice the difference between using muscular force and intent. As soon as you have understood the difference, you have something to build on. Use an attitude of experimentation. Play with the exercise and see what you can get out of it. The biggest failures normally happen with macho types who try to exert their full strength in one sudden shot. Work gradually, and you will succeed.

Using Muscular Force

The object is for your partner to try to bend your arm at the elbow. He or she should apply pressure gently to avoid injury. Try to make sure that you are evenly matched in size!

1. Stand opposite each other. Put your arm on your partner's shoulder. Clench your fist and tense the muscles in your arm.

2. Let your partner know when you are ready. He or she will then apply pressure to your elbow.

3. You are in a weak position, so your elbow will gradually collapse.

Using Your Intent

You have just tried the exercise using your muscles; you will now try it using your mind.

1. Stand opposite each other as before, with your arm on your partner's shoulder. This time, keep your palm open and your muscles relaxed. Imagine that your fingers are extending. Visualize invisible extensions coming from your fingers through the walls of the building, through the Earth's atmosphere, and past the solar system so that they can "tickle the stars."

2. When you have visualized extensions, give your partner a nod. Your partner will then start to apply pressure gradually. As you feel the pressure, do not tense your muscles. Instead, imagine that their force is being transmitted to the stars with your intent. Be a little stubborn. Tell yourself that your partner will not bend your arm and that the force is being redirected far outward.

If you have managed to hold the position, feel the muscles in your arm. If they are loose, you are using intent, which is correct. If your muscles are tense, you are using muscular force, so rethink the exercise and try again. If you are really having difficulties, a good instructor can sometimes help by moving a little energy for you.

It is not important to see how much force you can hold. What is important is to feel the difference between using your muscles and your intent.

Grounding

In the English language, we have phrases like "he knows how to keep both feet on the ground" or "she is a well-grounded type of person." This is usually intended to be a compliment, meaning that although chaos may be happening around that person, he or she has the ability to maintain an inner calm and continue as normal. The opposite would be the type of person who is "up in the air" or a "loose cannon." That person has no stability and is unpredictable. The language of tai chi is very similar to these metaphors. The word "grounded" is used to describe a person who can perform the tai chi exercises in a strong and stable way.

As with all aspects of tai chi and qi gong, the mind and the body are inseparable. If your tai chi has the aspect of solidity that is given by good grounding, then your mind is focused and not flying off at a tangent at every opportunity.

Good grounding is the platform from which all meditation starts. Even in the most esoteric of meditation systems, the first stage of training is usually some kind of mental and spiritual grounding. Without this initial preparation it can be difficult, or even dangerous, to try to reach some of the higher levels of meditation.

In tai chi, the footwork should be solid. Do not confuse this with rigidity of movement. A tai chi master's movement is very soft and smooth. However, when he or she demonstrates the martial aspects of the movements, it is like being hit by a bus!

The overextended position shown on the left is less grounded than the position shown on the right.

Most of the skills, such as softness and balance, in tai chi can be practiced individually, and grounding is no exception. You will need a partner to push and pull you about. This provides a good way of testing your postures and building up your strength. If you practice with a sense of fun, you will stand more chance of getting it right and enjoying yourself.

When testing, help your partner. Do not suddenly apply force. It would be difficult for anybody to withstand the force of 154 to 176 pounds (70 to 80 kilograms) of human flying at him or her without flinching! Besides, in tai chi,

you would turn to deflect the movement instead of trying to meet it head-on. The exercises are teaching you strength within your frame, not how to be the strongest person on the planet.

Apply force gradually. Remember that you are both learning from the exercise. Find your partner's limits and see if you can help him or her to extend them. Practicing slowly and gradually allows you to build the technique. Sudden movements may result in injury.

We will now look at some simple grounding exercises. They are based on stances and positions that have either been discussed previously or are developments of what you already know.

Standing-like-a-tree Exercise

You already know this exercise. Here we test the posture by pushing from all sides. This is not a position that is spectacularly strong unless you are already quite skilled, but it is very good for strengthening and straightening your posture. It is good to practice the testing exercise fairly regularly, especially for the beginner.

1. Start in the standing-like-a-tree position.

2. Your partner should then push you from behind, gradually applying force to your sacrum. Feel the force and try to sink the push through your legs. You may need to adjust your position slightly—this is part of the learning process.

3. Your partner should then push from a higher position at the back of your head. Keep your chin down and dig in with your legs. You will feel the force being grounded through your legs. This exercise forces you to hold your back straight. If you are leaning, you will not be able to hold the force.

4. Try the same exercise again, this time with your partner pushing both the back of your head and your sacrum. (This exercise is very good for opening the spine.) Remember to apply pressure gradually if you are doing the pushing, otherwise you may injure your partner.

5. Now try the push from the front. If you are being pushed, keep your shoulders down and try to ground the force through your legs.

6. When you have tried the exercise from the front, try it from the sides. Keep your knees bent and sink onto your legs. If your partner finds it easy to push you, it is because you are not grounded. If you know that you can do better, and that you have not simply reached your limit, try calming your mind before making a second attempt.

If you have another person on hand, try the exercise with one pushing from either side. If you can manage the first parts of the exercise, it is fun to play with this idea.

Bow-stance Exercise

The horse-riding stance is a good position in which to start with your grounding exercises because it is the most straightforward. To practice grounding in the bow stance, we will apply exactly the same logic as we did when practicing the horse-riding stance (page 75).

1. Go into the bow stance (see page 76). Push your arms out as though you were trying to push an automobile. Keep your arms straight, but do not lock your elbows and keep your shoulders down. This is called the two-handed-push position. It is probably the easiest position in which to test your grounding. When you can hold a good force in this posture, try others like ward off (see page 121) and press (see pages 122 to 123). Remember that the key to the horse-riding stance was to keep your back straight. Check that your back is straight now and that your torso lines up with your rear leg. Extend your arms as you did for the unbreakable-arm exercise (see pages 96 to 98).

2. Your partner should now gradually apply pressure to your hands until you cannot hold it any more.

Where was it that your position collapsed? If, for example, it was your shoulders, then your shoulders were the weakest part of your stance. Try adjusting your shoulders (sink them into a lower position) and try again. You can always use this approach to find the weakest part of your stance. Eventually, when all of the weak parts have been smoothed out, you will be able to withstand the force of many people pushing you.

This exercise teaches you how to withstand a push, but it could be that you need to withstand a pull. Try the exercise

again, but this time with your partner pulling instead of pushing. Make sure that your shin is held vertically so that you can sink the energy of your partner's pull into your front leg.

Being primarily for forward attacks, the bow stance is strongest in the forward direction. However, it would be virtually useless if it could not withstand a force from the side. Try the exercise again, with your partner pushing from the side. If it is easy to push you, your stance may be too narrow. Your feet should be shoulder-width apart. Readjust them and try again.

Empty Stance

It is quite hard work to stand in the empty stance for a long time. By performing grounding in the other stances first, you should be able to apply the exercise to the empty stance more quickly and less painfully.

1. Start in the empty stance, with your palm outstretched. Remember to "tickle the stars."

2. Your partner should then push against your hand. Keep adjusting yourself until you can withstand a strong push. Do not forget that it may take weeks, or even months, before you can do this.

Try the same exercise with a pull. If it is easy to pull you, look at the position of your leading, empty leg. When your partner pulls, his or her effort is grounded via this leg. The angle of the knee therefore needs to be greater than 90 degrees, otherwise you will just topple over.

Feeling the Chi

So far, we have performed exercises that move chi around the body. If you are sensitive, or have been practicing for a while, you may have experienced the movement of chi. For some (myself included), an exercise that gives you a feeling of "that's it!" is encouraging when trying to work out if you are actually "feeling the chi."

If you do not get it at once, it does not mean that there is anything wrong. Be open to the experience. This does not mean trying to force the experience. (How can an experimenter try to force a result?) Part of the experimentation process is to see what happens.

The "force field" between your hands is chi. Play with it. Move your hands and see how far apart they can go without losing the chi connection.

If the exercise worked, you now have the basic tool for including energy in your tai chi work. You are on the way to becoming a tai chi master!

1. Start with any exercise that moves chi, such as the standing-like-a-tree exercise. Perform the exercise for a short while until you think that you have moved chi.

2. Stand in a relaxed position and slowly bring your hands together. At a certain point you will feel the influence of the other hand. For me, it feels like two magnets repelling each other, but others feel different sensations, such as heat.

Softness and Sensitivity

According to the Taoist world view, the idea of yin and yang applies to everything. This implies that everything has either a yin or yang quality, depending upon what you are comparing it to.

The notion of being grounded is about establishing a degree of solidity in your movements. If this were too extreme, you would probably become so grounded in a fixed position that you could not actually move out of it. The solid, yang quality of being grounded must therefore be tempered with a yin quality.

A yin quality that fits the bill is the idea of softness. If you can learn how to be soft, it will increase your sensitivity, and if you learn how to be more sensitive, you will improve your softness.

Tai chi is famous for its softness because it is developed to such a high level. One of the strategies in tai chi is to use your softness to absorb and redirect an attack. The way it works is that if an attack comes to you, it is not always necessary to deflect it. If you deflect it, then your opponent can attack again. If you are so soft that your opponent can hardly feel your touch, he or she will not withdraw the attack unless the person is very alert. By encouraging the attack to come to you, you have the advantage because you know where it is going. You can then use your opponent's force to throw him or her. This is a high skill level that requires softness, sensitivity, and good grounding.

Developing Softness

The first thing to realize about being soft is that it is not being inert. Your body is filled with intent, and softness needs to be developed like any other skill. An important aspect of softness is to be able to relax your body. The level of relaxation that we are looking for will not happen overnight. The tension in your body (we all have it) was probably built up over many years. There may be psychological and physiological aspects to your tension. Keep doing tai chi exercises, and this will gradually improve.

Because many people hold tension in their shoulders, a good place to start is with the shoulders. Try the following exercise.

Ask your partner to hold the weight of your outstretched hand.

Without signaling, your partner should then suddenly take their hand away and remove their support.

What happened? There are three possibilities that I have encountered, as follows.

1. Your arm hardly moved. This means that you have tension in your shoulders. You need to "let go" of your arm and allow it to fall. If you find this difficult, ask your partner to give your shoulders a massage. This can help to relieve tension.

2. Your arm moved about halfway and then stopped. This means that you are in the halfway stage of relaxing your shoulders. Try to let your shoulders go so that your arm can drop completely.

3. Your arm dropped to your side. This means that your shoulders are fairly soft. There could still be tension deep down, but you are getting the idea of releasing your shoulders.

Try the same exercise with your leg. Ask your partner to hold up your leg and see how easy it is to let your knee go.

Relaxation

One of the processes of tai chi is letting go of tension. This is a mental process as much as a physical process. A way of working with the mental side of relaxation is through meditation. Try the following meditation exercise for relaxation.

This meditation exercise is useful for anybody who wants to reduce stress. The only difficulty with it is that you can become so relaxed that you fall asleep! If this happens, do not think that you are missing out. If you fall asleep quickly, your body probably needs sleep. If you have relaxed your body and mind with the meditation, it can help your sleep to be very refreshing. If you are worried about sleeping too long, set an alarm clock. Conversely, this exercise is useful for those nights when you are tired, but cannot sleep. If you do not go to sleep, you enter a state of deep relaxation that will usually lead to sleep unless you consciously stop the process.

1. Lie on a flat surface, with a little support under your head so that your spine is straight. (This is the corpse position in yoga.) Spread and relax your fingers and position your arms slightly away from your body. Close your eyes.

2. Imagine that your body is made of layers, like the layers of an onion or the rings of a tree. These layers are the layers of tension that you are about to dissolve.

3. Feel the skin on your forehead. Imagine the skin becoming more relaxed as you let go of your tension. Imagine that the tension is just draining away like water. Extend the feeling with your mind so that the tension drains away from your face and scalp. Spend a few minutes doing this. Tension can be stored in the face, and now is your chance to release it.

4. Move your mind through your body, using your imagination to release the tension in your neck, shoulders, arms, torso, legs, and, finally, your feet.

5. Bring your attention back to your forehead and start the process again. This time, imagine that you are working a layer deeper. You do not have much flesh to work on with the forehead, but as you move through your face, imagine that your facial muscles are relaxing. Move down the rest of your body. Imagine that you are like one of the diagrams that you see in anatomy books and that each of your muscles is relaxing. Finish with the tendons and muscles in your toes. If your muscles start to twitch, it is normally because they are releasing tension. If this becomes too uncomfortable, stop the exercise.

6. Bring your mind back up to your head again. The next layer down is the skull. Try to imagine that the plates of your skull are relaxing and that tension is actually being released from the bones. Move your mind through the rest of your skeleton. Allow your bones to relax. If you experience strange sensations, take note of how they feel and try to release the tension in that area. Pay special attention to each of the vertebrae.

7. The next level concerns the organs in your body. Imagine that your brain is actually relaxing physically. Actually "feeling" your brain relax may seem like a strange idea, but use your imagination. Move down your spinal cord and into your organs. Imagine that your lungs, liver, stomach, intestines, and all of the other organs are relaxing. If you have made it this far without falling asleep or being distracted, you have entered a very deep state of relaxation. Do not be too surprised if emotions bubble to the surface. Try to let the feelings pass. If you cannot, gently revive yourself.

8. Nine out of ten people will have fallen asleep before step 7. This is fine. As your body and mind become more relaxed, you will have more energy at your disposal and will be able to relax more deeply. If you have reached the organ level, or have simply gone as far as you want to go, try to hold the state for a while. Profound healing can take place on an emotional and physical level if you allow your body to relax this much.

9. When you have finished, gently revive yourself. Take it easy for a few minutes and allow yourself to return to the normal world. Sipping a glass of water can be very helpful. The same applies if you fell asleep—just go easy on yourself.

Microcosmic Orbit

The microcosmic-orbit meditation joins the two meridians that run through the center of your body. The meridian in your back runs over the top of your spine and is commonly called the governing vessel. The meridian that runs through the front of your body is called the conception vessel. These meridians are important because all of the other meridians in the body are internally linked to them. Moving energy through the meridian loop described will therefore have a positive effect on all of the meridians.

This meditation is useful as a sitting meditation or can be brought into your tai chi or qi gong practice when you have gained enough experience to make it easy. Indeed, some Taoist schools, such as the Healing Tao run by Master Mantak Chi, use this meditation as a fundamental building block for further practice.

In the beginning, you may find that you do not feel much. The biggest mistake is either to dismiss the exercise or to try to rush it. Both will prevent you from succeeding. Taking it easy and going easy on yourself will lead to success.

1. Sit in a comfortable, cross-legged position. Use a pillow if that makes you feel more comfortable. It is important that your position is comfortable because any discomfort will distract you from the

meditation. There is no need to assume the lotus or half-lotus position for this particular meditation.

2. Sit with your back straight and your chin tucked down. This will stop your head from tipping backward and will keep the upper half of your spine straight. Place your hands in a comfortable position, such as on your abdomen.

3. Put your tongue on the roof of your mouth. This acts like a light switch, connecting the governing vessel and the conception vessel.

4. Start the abdominal breathing described on page 71.

5. On an inward breath, imagine that you are moving energy with your mind. Lift it from your perineum along your spine, to the top of your skull, and down to the roof of your mouth, where your tongue is touching it.

6. On the exhalation, let the energy travel through your tongue, down your throat, through the middle of your sternum, through the middle of your abdomen, through the sex organs, and finally finish at the perineum.

7. This is your first cycle of the microcosmic-orbit meditation. Continue this breathing pattern. Remember to lift on the inward breath and to release on the outward breath.

8. For maximum benefit, this exercise should be performed for as long as is comfortable. Five to ten minutes is all right for the beginner, but it becomes more interesting when you continue for longer periods of time. When you are ready, finish the exercise by bringing the energy to your tan tien and circulating it in that area for a few breaths. This helps you to stay grounded.

Healing with Tai Chi

Throughout the history of tai chi, many of the masters have been experts in such healing arts as acupuncture and shiatsu. Even the masters who were not particularly inclined toward these healing arts would have had a basic understanding of them. In fact, many martial arts masters, such as Sun Lu Tang (see pages 48 to 49), regarded the healing aspect of the martial arts to be more important than the fighting aspect.

This is an interesting concept. Having practiced for a certain amount of time, a student will start to gain martial skill, and this will normally be tested in some way. The testing could be sparring, pushing-hand, or form competitions. At first, the student will go to a teacher who offers advice on the technique. When the same question has been asked enough times, the student will start to look inside herself rather than looking to the teacher for solutions.

This kind of introspection is sometimes magnified by the physical and mental demands of the training. We train to meet a demand and a new set of challenges appears. By this time, we are no longer fighting an opponent: the battle has become internal. Winning or losing against an opponent is seen as an ego issue. Winning is not even seen as being particularly good. We learn far more from the person who can beat us every time. Eventually, we find a way of stopping them and an improvement is made.

Relaxation becomes an issue. If you are tense, the techniques in tai chi cannot work to their full extent. We use meditation techniques to try to dissolve tension on a mental level, as well as a physical one. We are no longer working with the body; we are working with the mind and the spirit. This is the transformational nature of tai chi. We start by learning crude, physical techniques and, through diligence and training, find that we need to strengthen the body to strengthen the mind, and that relaxation is the key to further improvement.

Some Taoists call this process "inner alchemy" because we are taking the base materials of the body and are using the spirit to transmute to something higher.

Chi Self-Massage

A useful technique for relaxing the body and helping both the circulation and the chi is self-massage. The sequence shown here uses a pounding technique for massaging the meridians and is quite invigorating.

For this reason, I recommend that you do not try it just before going to bed because it can wake up your body when you are trying to relax and wind down. Using the same logic, it is a good idea to perform the massage before breakfast. You will feel ready for anything that you face in your day.

As with all techniques in this book, try not to be too heavy-handed. Listen to your body, and if your body tells you to stop, follow its advice.

This massage sequence requires tapping with the fist. Keep your fist relaxed and do not tap too hard. Some medical conditions can be aggravated by this massage because it can stimulate the flow of lymph and can therefore distribute toxins. If you think that this may be harmful to you, consult an expert first. Each of the stages can be repeated as many times as you like: one or many times, the choice is yours.

1. Tap along the outside of your arm, moving in a line toward your index finger. Go back up your arm, following a line from your thumb to your inner shoulder. Tap on the outer midline, moving toward your middle finger.

Repeat the process along the inner midline of your arm. Now tap again down your outer arm, working in a line toward your little finger. Repeat the same tapping procedure on your inner arm.

2. Bend the elbow of the arm being tapped so that you can tap and massage your shoulder. Repeat the process on the other arm.

3. Tap your chest and abdomen with both hands.

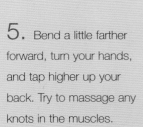

4. Bend forward and tap your buttocks.

5. Bend a little farther forward, turn your hands, and tap higher up your back. Try to massage any knots in the muscles.

6. Tap down the outside of your legs and then up the inner sides of your legs.

7. Try to cover all of the major muscle groups, but take care when working on your shins.

Know Your Back

In tai chi, we need to be able to understand our own backs. If we know how the muscles work in the back, we stand more of a chance of training properly. The reason for this is that power is transmitted through the back. If your back is weak or aligned poorly, then you cannot work to your full potential. This understanding need not always be intellectual. I could not tell you the names of all of the muscles, but I can tell you how a healthy back feels. This kind of understanding is what tai chi is all about, rather than learning with your mind and forgetting your body.

If you give a friend a basic back massage, you will learn how another person's back feels. He or she may have a strong or weak back. Learning about other people is a good way of learning more about yourself. If you try the following treatment on a friend, work gently. As long as you are careful and do not use excessive force, you should not cause injury. Do not try the treatment if you know that there is a problem. Leave that to the professionals.

Basic Treatment

Ask the person if he or she has any complaints that you need to know about. Remember, you are not a professional and do not have insurance for any damage caused. If there is a complaint, it is probably best to leave the area alone.

The person receiving the treatment should lie face down on the floor. A futon mattress is ideal to lie on, but if one is not available, try using a few blankets.

1. Kneel down next to the person. It is useful to keep an eye on his or her face. Sometimes a person will not tell you if you are hurting them, but their face will usually change. Kneel in a stable position so that you cannot fall on top of the person.

2. "Walk" your hands over the person's back. Make a good connection, but try not to be too rough.

3. Move along the body and up the other side so that you can massage the backs of the legs and the calves. Do not put pressure on the knee or ankle joint.

4. Come back to a position high up the person's back. Use your thumbs to press on either side of the spine, approximately half a hand-width apart. Press in the space between the ribs.

5. Work your way down the back to the sacrum. Place both hands on the sacrum and hold them there. The pressure need not be too heavy. Feel your contact with the other person.

6. Hold one hand on the sacrum and work the other hand down the center of the leg. If necessary, move your hand from the sacrum farther down the leg.

7. When you reach the ankle, work along the outside of the Achilles tendon and along the outer edge of the foot to the little toe. Repeat on the other leg.

"Eight Energies"

When I first heard about the "eight energies" in tai chi, my thoughts were along the lines of, "But I have only just started learning the first one," meaning chi. What I did not understand was that the eight energies are not actually new energies, but are different ways of understanding chi.

To start with, I viewed them as techniques rather than energies, and saw that all of the techniques within the tai chi repertoire were built from different blends of the eight energies or techniques. Reason told me that the eight energies were a vital aspect of tai chi. I chose movements from the tai chi form that emphasized each of the energies and practiced them for hours on end until the techniques became smooth and instinctive.

I then experienced a shift in perception. Rather than viewing the energies as techniques, I could see them more as concepts. I could see how they manifested themselves in other martial arts, such as judo, and could apply them to strategic games like chess and backgammon. The idea of describing these eight actions as techniques was starting to feel clumsy.

In the tai chi form, the energies constantly flow around each other. All movements use a combination of them. A good example is waving hands like clouds (see pages 87 to 89). It begins with ward off, follows with roll back, and finishes with a press. When you can express these in your movements, you will understand the difference between the energy and the technique.

Some readers may be making connections here: we have eight energies and eight trigrams in the I-Ching. A correlation has been made between the I-Ching hexagrams and the eight energies. Examples are that roll back corresponds to earth because you need to be rooted, and ward off corresponds to heaven because of the expansive feeling. This is really the realm of the advanced Taoist, however, and it is not necessary to analyze it further here.

A list of the eight energies with their Chinese names and I-Ching correspondences is shown opposite.

English	Chinese	I-Ching
1. Ward off	peng	heaven
2. Roll back	lu	earth
3. Press	ji	water
4. Push	an	fire
5. Pull down	tsai	wind
6. Split	lieh	thunder
7. Elbow stroke	jou	lake
8. Shoulder stroke	kao	mountain

Ward Off

Ward off is the primary technique in tai chi, hsing-i, and ba gua. In Chen-style tai chi, manuals describe ward off as the source of all of the other energies in tai chi.

The feeling of ward off is one of expansion. In the Yang-family manuscripts, T'an Meng-hsien describes the feeling as being like water supporting a moving boat. Others describe the feeling as the force that makes a cork float on water. The ideas of floating and buoyancy are common in descriptions of ward off.

If you are following the exercises in this book, you already know the feeling of ward off, and the standing-like-a-tree position is excellent for developing ward-off strength. Ward off can be used as a sudden expansion to give you room against an opponent, as a block to deflect an incoming blow, or as a strike.

It can also be soft, being used to intercept an attack without the attacker fully realizing that it has happened. If you practice tai chi, you will be working on your ward-off energy. If you actually understand the energy of ward off, your practice can become more focused.

At the start of the Yang-style tai chi form, there is a movement called ward off, which offers an excellent example of using the ward-off energy. Look at the posture and imagine how it could be used to suddenly explode or to intercept an attack gently.

Roll Back

In roll back, two points are moving together in a circle. The points can be your hands or two parts of a hand. It is important to understand using the points because this focuses your intent.

Some descriptions compare roll back to drawing silk. The idea is that the motion is coming toward you and that it is smooth. If you slow down, the silk will be uneven; if you suddenly speed up, the silk will snap.

In roll back, the opponent is allowed to advance. You follow the incoming force and draw it in until it overextends. As long as you have maintained a stable position, you will be in control. The roll-back technique does not rely on strength in the same way that ward off does. In roll back, we must be able to flow with our partner or opponent and sense the moment that we can force them to overextend. Sometimes this is called "sticking" because you stick to your opponent like a magnet.

Roll back can be used as a fast or fa-jing technique. This would normally involve an attack to a joint, such as the elbow, which would result in a dislocation or break if done forcefully. It can also be used to redirect and throw an attacker. The essence when trying to throw a person is timing. This makes your connection with the person and the timing of your movement vital.

A strong attack can be redirected and the attacker thrown by a very small person if roll back is used properly. There are many stories of senior tai chi masters throwing a young opponent across a room when they were attacked. There was no "magical" force involved. The tai chi master redirected the attacker's force using roll back. See grasping the sparrow's tail (pages 133 to 135) for examples of these techniques.

Press

If you have ever seen a snooker or pool player use the cue ball to strike two balls that are touching and only the second ball moves, you have seen press energy. Another example is the "Newton's cradle" toy, in which the momentum of one ball striking a line of balls in a row causes the end ball to move.

The press movement in tai chi is made by generating ward-off energy in the two arms and connecting them. This is used as a sudden expansion or a strike, and the combined energy of the two arms can be very powerful.

Following the laws of physics, if you are projecting forward powerfully, your body will want to follow the momentum, but this would not be good because you would be uprooting yourself. When using press, your legs therefore have to be strong and well rooted. This is also true if you actually strike something. The reaction from the impact can be enough to knock you over unless your legs are strong. For these reasons, you need to pay as much attention to your lower body as to your upper body in these techniques.

Press can be used simply to knock people out of the way or to attack a vital organ. Press can also be used as a defensive maneuver if you need a strong block. The movement is shown above; note how the arms are rounded in the ward-off shape and the legs are firmly placed.

Push

The energy of push is probably the easiest of the energies to understand. On a basic level, push is exactly what it says: a push. Examples are shown later for the two-handed push in the grasping-the-sparrow's-tail sequence (see pages 133 to 135) and the single-handed push from brush knee and twist.

As with all tai chi movements, there is a subtlety to the movement, and in this case it is about keeping softness within the push. If you were to push with a solid arm, you would still get the push. However, if you lock your arm to make it solid, it is easy to overextend the arm. If you are overextending, repeated practice can damage your elbow. Not only that, but if your arm is close to overextension, it is easy for an opponent to take advantage and attack your elbow. So your arm should be straight, but not locked.

If you go too far the other way and overemphasize the

softness, it becomes impossible to generate any power.

In order to achieve the push, use the same "unbreakable arm" that you used for ward off. The only difference between ward off and push is the hand position and the intent of your mind. Push should be rooted in your feet and come through your body like a wave. The wave should seek out the places of weakness and penetrate. If you have softness in your push, this is possible.

In the tai chi form, push is not always performed with an open hand. If you close your fist for a punch, you are still using push energy. If you kick with your heel, you are using push energy with your foot. In all cases, there should be softness within the hardness, and your feet (or foot, if you are kicking) should be the anchor of your power.

Pull Down

To understand pull down, grab hold of a towel and try cracking it like a whip. Make the "crack" quite powerful, and then take a look at the pattern that your hand is making. To get real power into the "crack," you draw your hand toward yourself and then suddenly flick it downward. If you miss the drawing-inward part, it is difficult to get such a good flick.

Now think of this in terms of the energies. You are drawing the towel inward. This would be roll back. You are then quickly applying a downward force. This is push. This combination of roll back and downward push is called pull down.

The pull down described is an extreme version. If you imagine that you had a hold of someone's hand when you made the maneuver, you could imagine causing whiplash injuries or dislocations. This was a popular technique for Sun Lu Tang (see pages 48 to 49), and is therefore common in the Sun-style tai chi routine.

Another variation would be to draw out the attacker's arm and press down in a less violent way. If you imagine an outstretched fist and your hand pressing down on it, you would not need to exert much pressure to force the arm downward. You are using the leverage of your attacker's arm

against him. If this is coupled with an upward movement from your other arm, you are performing the common strum-the-lute movement.

Split

If you have ever thrown a Frisbee, then you have used "split" energy. This is the basic movement behind the part-the-wild-horse's-mane movement shown below. If you were to throw something onto a wheel that is spinning fairly quickly, the motion of the wheel flicks whatever it was that you threw away from it. This is how split energy works.

In engineering, this energy is called centrifugal force. It acts away from the center of movement. Your waist is like a flywheel and your arm is thrown outward, from your waist. This "throwing" can be done on any plane. In the part-the-wild-horse's-mane movement, it is on a horizontal plane. If you were to use split on a vertical plane, you would get a movement like white crane spreads its wings.

Split energy is used if your hands are moving in

opposite directions. This can be looked upon as using the ward-off and push energies simultaneously.

In the example of part the wild horse's mane, the leading arm is used for the attack. This is an example of using ward off for a strike. The other arm presses downward. The downward press gives more power to the striking arm and helps with the ever-important grounding. Split can be used as a strike or as a way of moving your opponent (normally for a throw). This depends upon the timing and intent that you are using.

Elbow Stroke

In martial arts, it is often said that there are three layers of attack. The farthest out is the reach of the hands and feet; the middle distance is the elbow and knees; and the inner attack layer is the shoulder and torso.

For the mid-layer of attack, tai chi uses the elbow stroke. The elbow stroke is useful when dealing with an opponent who is good at kicking and

punching because he or she will be vulnerable to a close-range attack.

In this situation, you have to be brave! A good way to deal with your opponent is to go inside his or her range of attack. This means going so close to your opponent that there is no room for him or her to kick or punch you.

The disadvantage of doing this is that you also have no room in which to kick or punch back. This sounds like an ideal opportunity to use your elbow.

The elbow is very powerful. It is not as fast-moving as a kick or a punch, but has more torque. As you move closer to your opponent's body, your speed of attack becomes slower, but the attack becomes more powerful. Elbows can be used in any plane of movement: up, down, sideways, or slanting. The elbow is not limited to the elbow strike (see pages 213 to 214): it can be used as a block, as a pivot point for a limb lock, or to press into a pressure point.

Shoulder Stroke

A good example of shoulder stroke is in the Yang-style tai chi form in the transition between raise hands and white crane spreads its wings.

In shoulder stroke, the whole torso of the body is used for the attack. The technique, when applied properly, is very powerful. When I first had shoulder stroke demonstrated on me, it felt like my whole body was being jarred and that my teeth would smash! A common mistake that some people make is using the shoulder like a battering ram. While this may be powerful, it means that your body tilts and that you consequently lose your center.

Tai Chi Styles

It is unwise for the beginner to try to learn all of the tai chi styles. However, having an understanding of the different styles, along with hsing-i and ba gua, will increase your tai chi vocabulary.

Tai Chi Forms

A major component of any tai chi syllabus is what is called the "tai chi form." The "form" is a set sequence of movements that is designed to teach students the essence of their chosen style.

Tai chi is not unique in its use of forms or patterns. Virtually every martial art uses them as a teaching tool. As with other martial arts, the tai chi form is only a part of the syllabus, giving you the opportunity to show what you have done to develop your skill in a fixed pattern.

The fixed pattern gives you a reference point. You can gain a better idea of your skill level by repeating the same sequence than by constantly changing your sequences. If you practice one set of moves one day and change it the next, it is very difficult to judge whether you are improving. If you extend the time to a year, you should see a good improvement. However, if your patterns are constantly changing, you do not know exactly what you did a year ago, so you have nothing to measure your progress against.

For this reason, the tai chi forms are sometimes used in competitions. The competitor will demonstrate his or her form to a panel of judges, who will give a mark depending on the quality within the form. Again, tai chi is not unique in employing this method.

One way in which tai chi forms do usually differ from other martial styles is that the patterns are longer and are performed more slowly. There are many reasons for practicing slowly. The most obvious one is the way in which your muscles need to work. It is more difficult to execute a movement slowly than it is quickly. If you are doubtful of this, try performing a good, high kick at normal kicking speed. Then try to do the same at a slow speed. Other reasons for working slowly are that you can concentrate on your timing and that it allows changes to occur within your body. If you can work in a slow way, then your body will relax into the movement.

We will not try to study all of the styles of tai chi here, but will look at the opening movements of the Yang-style and Chen-style forms, these being the most common; we will take a look at some of the movements from hsing-i and ba gua, the "sisters" of tai chi; and we will also take a look at some other tai chi movements, both with and without weapons.

The intention is not specifically to teach you all of the movements: you need a teacher to learn them properly. If you follow the movements through, however, this will give you a flavor of the different styles and how tai chi theory works with them.

Yang-style Tai Chi Form: First Section

The Yang-style tai chi form is sometimes called the "long form." Depending on how you count the movements, there can be over one hundred in total. The form itself is structured in three sections. The first section teaches the basics, the second section teaches you new ways of looking at the basics, and the third section teaches you something of the complexity that is hidden within tai chi.

The sequence is usually performed slowly. There is nothing stopping you from experimenting with fa-jing (fast) movements, but if you are doing the whole form, it is better to keep your movements slow. Depending on your style of practicing, the full form can take from twenty to forty-five minutes to complete.

Opening Form

1. Start in the wu chi position (see page 73). Relax your body and mind. Keep your back straight and your shoulders relaxed, with your arms hanging in front of you.

2. Extend your fingers downward.

3. Then point them forward.

6. Finally, press down with your palms. When your hands are level with the tan-tien point in your abdomen, bend your knees and sink your weight downward.

5. On the inhalation, lower your shoulders, elbows, and forearms.

4. On the exhalation, thrust your fingers forward until they are at shoulder height.

Ward Off Left

1. Shift your weight onto your left leg so that you can turn your right foot through 45 degrees. Pivot on your heel. Turn your body with the movement.

2. Shift your weight back onto your right leg.

3. Then step forward with your left leg to make a bow stance. Extend your left arm as you step forward into the ward-off position.

Grasping the Sparrow's Tail

1. Shift your weight onto your right leg so that you can turn your left foot through 45 degrees. Relax your left forearm.

2. When you have turned your left foot, shift your weight back onto it.

3. Step forward with your right leg.

4. Make a bow stance. Your arms should be in the ward-off position shown above.

5. Extend your arms in the ward-off transition.

6. Shift your weight back onto your left leg for the roll-back position.

7. Drop your hands in front of your body and turn your torso ready for the press position.

8. Push from your left leg to extend into the press position.

9. Shift your weight back onto your left leg and separate your hands.

10. Push from your left leg to extend into the push position.

Single Whip

1. Sink your weight onto your left leg and turn your waist. Let your arms come naturally toward your center.

2. Push outward with both hands and adjust the position of your right foot.

3. Draw your hands inward and turn your waist.

6. Extend both arms and push your left foot forward in the bow stance.

5. Step forward with your left foot into a bow stance. As you are stepping, draw your hand toward your center.

4. Shift your weight onto your right leg as you push outward. Make a hook with your right hand and a ward-off shape with your left hand. Release your left heel so that you can step forward.

Raise Hands

1. Turn through 90 degrees to your left, then adjust the position of your left foot.

2. Position your right foot in the empty stance and then bring your hands together simultaneously.

White Crane Spreads Its Wings

1. Turn your waist to the left. Pull back with your left hand and press down with your right hand.

2. Step forward with your right leg and split with your forearms for a shoulder stroke.

3. Shift your weight onto your right leg. As you transfer your weight, use the momentum of your body's movement to separate your arms. Your left hand should finish by your side and your right hand should be raised.

Brush and Push

1. Rotate your body to the left and drop your right hand downward. Rotate your left hand.

2. Pull back with your right elbow and rotate your body in such a way that your left forearm protects your center line.

3. Step forward into the bow stance with your left leg. Raise your right hand and lower your left hand.

4. Shift your weight into the bow stance. Push forward with your right hand and down with your left.

Strum the Lute

1. Move your right knee forward.

2. Shift into the empty stance, with your weight on your right leg. As your weight moves downward, execute the pull-down movement by pulling downward with your right hand and thrusting upward with your left hand.

Brush and Push Three Times

For this movement, we will use the tai chi walk that we practiced earlier (see pages 80 to 81), coupled with the brush-and-push movement demonstrated on page 140.

1. Step forward into the bow stance with your left leg and push with your right hand (first push).

2. Shift back onto your right leg and turn your body. Turn your left foot 45 degrees.

3. Shift your weight onto your left leg and step forward with your right for a bow stance.

4. Shift your weight onto your leading, right leg and push forward with your left hand and down with your right (second push).

5. Shift back onto your left leg and turn your right foot through 45 degrees.

6. Shift your weight onto your right leg and step forward with your left leg for a bow stance.

7. Push through with your right hand while pushing your weight forward onto your left leg (third push).

Strum the Lute

This strum-the-lute movement is identical to the one shown on page 141.

2. Shift into the empty stance, with your weight on your right leg. As your weight moves downward, execute the pull-down movement by pulling downward with your right hand and thrusting upward with your left hand.

1. Move your right knee forward.

Brush and Push

A repetition of the brush-and-push movement shown on page 140. The Yang family obviously thought the movement fundamental to their style of tai chi because it dominates the first section of their form and continues to feature in the advanced sections.

Step forward with your left leg into the bow stance and push with your right hand.

Parry, Block, and Punch

1. Shift back onto your right leg, make a fist with your right hand, and open your left hand. Turn your left foot through 45 degrees.

2. Step forward with your left leg and lower both hands.

3. Put your right heel down, with your foot at a 45-degree angle. As your foot lands, raise your hands.

4. Step forward with your left foot, simultaneously pushing out your left hand.

5. Drive your right fist forward from your right heel. Finish with your left hand protecting your inner elbow.

Apparent Close-up

1. Rotate both forearms so that they face upward.

2. Shift downward, onto your right leg. Simultaneously pull back with your left elbow and sweep outward with your left hand.

3. Turn your waist and prepare your hands for a push.

4. Now push with both hands.

Closing Form

1. Turn your waist and left foot through 90 degrees. Simultaneously open your hands.

2. Bring your feet into the horse-riding stance and cross your arms in front of your body.

3. Extend your arms forward and separate them.

4. Press down with your hands, keeping your knees bent, until they are level with your tan-tien point.

5. When your hands reach the tan-tien level, straighten your legs. Release your hands and relax.

Chen-style Tai Chi Form: First Section

Many of the movements in the Chen-style tai chi form have the same, or similar, names to movements in the Yang-style tai chi form. When you look at two movements with the same name, they may look vaguely familiar, but are definitely different movements. The reason for this is that the movements use the same energies. If you remember your tai chi history, the Yang style derives from the Chen style. When the Yang style was invented, the same basic movements were used, but were applied in different ways.

This change in application altered the basic frame of the Yang-style form. In general, the Chen-style movements use longer stances than the Yang-style equivalents and the circular movements are bigger.

The Chen style is very intricate, with some fast movements and some slow ones. There are different versions of the Chen-style forms. The movements here are from the beginning of the Chen-style thirty-eight-movement form. Chen Xiaowang is a modern-day tai chi master and winner of many tai chi championships. He compiled the thirty-eight-movement form by combining elements of the Chen old frame (lao jia) and new frame (xin jia).

Preparing Form

1. The Chen-style form starts in the same way as the Yang-style form, except that the legs are slightly wider than shoulder-width apart. In the Yang-style form, they are shoulder-width apart.

2. Raise your hands to shoulder level. As your hands rise, your knees bend slightly and your body drops down.

3. Lower your hands and sink into the posture.

Buddha's Warrior Attendant Pounds Mortar

1. Shift a little of your weight onto your right leg. As you move, start to raise your palms in a twisting motion. Your left palm should lead the right.

2. Keep pressing down onto your right leg as your hands continue their upward journey.

3. Your right palm should finish about level with your shoulder, facing outward. Your left palm should be facing outward.

4. Turn your body to the right and shift your weight onto your left leg. Open your right foot.

5. Sink onto your right foot and raise your left knee. Do not lift it too high.

10. Stamp your right foot as you strike your right fist into the palm of your left hand. This movement is usually done with power, but can also be practiced slowly if circumstances dictate it.

9. Form a fist with your right hand and raise it at the same time as your right knee.

8. Step through with your right leg and touch your toe on the floor. Follow through with your left hand.

7. Push your left knee forward into a long bow stance. Your left hand should move down and your right hand should open.

6. Extend your left leg forward and touch down with your heel.

White Crane Spreads Its Wings

1. Shift your weight onto your right leg. Raise your right hand and press down with your left hand.

2. Shift your weight back onto your left leg and sink down onto it. As you sink, extend your right leg at a 45-degree angle and cross your arms in front of your chest. Your left arm should be in front of your right arm.

3. Turn your right foot through an angle of 45 degrees and shift your weight from your left to your right leg. Expand your elbows outward.

4. Bring your left foot inward and touch the floor with your toe. Press down with your left hand and upward with your right.

Hsing-i, the Five-element Style

As we discussed in the history of tai chi, Sun Lu Tang was one of the most influential figures in the internal Chinese arts. He invented the Sun style of tai chi, but his hsing-i training heavily influenced it.

Sun Lu Tang regarded the tai chi styles, together with the hsing-i and ba gua, as forming a trinity of martial arts. The operation of the styles is different, but the goal is the same. They are like different paths leading up the same mountain.

Sun Lu Tang was not the only martial artist to mix the styles. Throughout history, the styles have crossed over a lot. It is therefore educational for any student of tai chi to understand a little of the mechanics of how the other styles work.

Hsing-i is known for the directness of the attack. For this reason, it is sometimes incorrectly assumed that all movement is in straight lines. In many of the movements, you will turn your body in a similar way to tai chi. The timing is a little different, but the result is similar: you prevent somebody from hitting you!

In hsing-i, there are five sets of movements based on the five elements and twelve movements based on animals, with linking forms for both the elements and the animals. The animals in hsing-i describe the character of the movement. For example, the routine for the bear is very strong and grounded, while the routine for the eagle is fierce and violent. Some of the animals, such as the dragon, are based on mythical properties. Here we look at the basic movements for the five elements. This is the starting point for hsing-i practice and will help you to develop internal strength.

San Ti

San ti is the posture upon which all movement in hsing-i is based. The name

"san ti" means "trinity." The trinity is heaven, Earth, and the human being. In the posture, this relates to the head, hands, and feet.

San ti training is an important part of hsing-i practice. In the old days of China, it was normal for the hsing-i student to be taught nothing but the san ti posture for a year, having to work on it until perfection was reached.

If you are serious about learning hsing-i, this posture should be the basis of your training. The recommendation from the masters is that you should build up your strength gradually until you can stand in the position for one hour. With most people, this will take at least a year, depending on how much practice you do.

If you look at the posture, it is superficially very similar to the empty stance in tai chi. For the san ti posture, we need three vertical lines: the first is from the heel of the foot of the front leg to the knee of the front leg—a line from the kneecap should meet the heel; the second is a straight line from the hips to the heel of the foot of the rear leg; the third line is from the front hand to the front foot.

The weight distribution will happen naturally if the three verticals are correct. The majority of your weight should be on your back leg. As in tai chi postures, your head should be up, your neck straight, and your shoulders down. Your intention should be like a tiger ready to pounce.

Pi Quan: the Splitting Fist of Metal Energy

The splitting fist belongs to the metal element, as does the lung. This motion is characteristic of the metal element. Think of a hand falling like an ax. Below is a complete movement for the splitting fist. To continue, follow the same instructions, alternating between left and right.

1. Start in the san ti posture, with your weight on your left leg.

2. Open your left foot by 45 degrees and draw your fist inward.

3. Move your fist along the path of your center line until it is level with your throat.

4. Push your weight forward, onto your left leg, and thrust your fist outward.

5. Open your left hand and cross your forearms.

6. Take a step forward.

7. Smash downward with your right hand and draw back with your left hand.

8. As your hands open, your forearms can rub against each other.

Beng Quan: the Smashing Fist of Wood Energy

The organ for beng quan is the liver because the liver is ruled by wood energy. The smashing fist is like firing an arrow. The motion is produced through stretching and contracting.

1. Start in the san ti posture.

2. Make fists with both of your hands and soften your left elbow.

3. Your left fist should come back to the tan tien. Twist your waist to pull your left fist back and drive your right fist forward.

4. Repeat the movement, keeping your right leg as the standing leg. You should catapult your body from the right leg to drive your left fist forward. The fist then returns to the tan tien.

Zuan Quan: the Drilling Fist of Water Energy

The drilling fist flows like water. It can seep through the smallest hole and come crashing forward like a wave. The organ for the drilling fist is the kidney. This is a powerful movement that can cover large distances quickly. To repeat the movement, follow the same instructions, alternating between left and right.

1. Start in the san ti posture.

2. Open with your left leg and simultaneously make fists with both hands while rotating your wrists.

3. Push forward with your left leg as your forearms meet.

4. Finished.

Pao Quan: the Pounding Fist of Fire

This fist movement is sometimes called the "cannon fist" because it is shot out like a cannon ball. The organ for pao quan is the heart.

1. Start in the san ti posture.

2. Step forward into the bow stance, with your left leg leading. Make "tiger claws" with your hands.

3. Form your hands into fists and pull them back to your abdomen. Draw your right foot toward your left.

4. Step at a 45-degree angle into the san ti position. Punch with your right hand and block upward with your left hand.

5. Step forward with your left leg and make fists with your hands.

6. Draw your right foot in, toward your left foot, and pull your fists toward your abdomen. Repeat step 4 on the other side.

The stepping for pao quan and the next movement, heng quan, follows the same sequence: a step at a 45-degree angle, followed by a forward step.

Heng Quan: the Crossing Fist of Earth

The crossing fist is round and solid in shape and therefore belongs to the earth element. The organs for the earth element are the stomach and spleen. Repeat this sequence as many times as you like.

1. Start in the san ti posture.

2. Step 45 degrees to your left in the san ti posture. Punch forward with your right fist and withdraw your left fist to your tan tien.

3. Keep your hands where they are and step forward with your left leg. Finish with your weight on your left leg and your right foot touching the ground. Turn 45 degrees to the right into the san ti posture. Punch with your left hand

Ba Gua

A little understanding of ba gua will complete our trinity of the internal martial art styles. In very general terms, tai chi is known for its use of softness to redirect a force, hsing-i for a direct and powerful attack, and ba gua for its evasion skills.

This certainly does not mean that the other elements are missing from each style. For example, hsing-i and tai chi have sophisticated and practical evasion skills, just as tai chi includes very powerful attacks. These generalizations have been made over the years to give an initial indication of what the style is mostly about.

The defining action of ba gua is "circle-walking." This can be done in a clockwise or a counterclockwise direction. There are many levels of circle-walking, and we will only cover the basic levels here.

- The first level: this is simply walking the circle with no arm actions, and is akin to the tai chi walk described earlier. It teaches you the most basic ba gua footwork.

- The second level: this is walking the circle with the arms in a fixed position, and is the same as the standing postures in tai chi and hsing-i. It is primarily aimed at developing power. The practitioner walks the circle as in the first level, but with the arms in a fixed position.

- The third level: this is walking with palm changes. This is a multilayered level. Basically, the ba gua student walks the circle while making the palm changes. This means that you will change between the eight fixed positions in ba gua while walking the circle. To gain any skill at this level, or the higher levels derived from it, you will need to spend a lot of time with a good teacher. Some of the palm changes are subtle and lose their impact if their subtleties are ignored.

Walking the Circle: the Straight Line

In ba gua, straight-line walking is very similar to tai chi walking, in that the feet are kept at a distance of shoulder-width apart and the weight is transferred from one leg to the other. The difference is in the way that you use your waist. In the tai chi walk, you turn your waist to open your toes. In ba gua walking, you keep your feet parallel, waist rotations happening only by transferring your weight from one leg to the other. Also note that the feet stay closer to the floor than in tai chi, and move parallel to it.

1. Start with your feet positioned shoulder-width apart.

2. Sink downward, keeping your back straight.

3. Shift your weight onto your left leg and move your right leg forward. It should hover about $3/4$ inch (2 cm) above the floor.

4. When you reach the end of your stride, put your right leg onto the floor.

5. Transfer your weight to your right leg. Step forward with your left leg in the same way that you did with your right.

Walking Turn in Ba Gua

Walking the straight line is a method of grounding your energy and trains you to sink your weight onto your legs. However, it is limited, and you need to be able to perform a 180-degree turn in order to keep practicing.

1. Shift your weight back onto your rear, left leg.

2. Bring your right foot around so that the toes of both feet point together in a knock-kneed-looking posture. Keep your knees soft and your back straight. This common ba gua stance is called "stepping inward."

3. Shift your weight onto your right leg. As you release the weight from your left leg, allow your waist to turn.

Circle-walking

So far, the basic steps in ba gua have not been particularly difficult. The same is true for the footwork for circle-walking. Yet experts train for years just trying to get the footwork correct. How can this be? There are many levels to the answer. The first reason is that the exercise trains your muscles. Just as in tai chi walking, you need to learn how to sink your weight onto your legs. To do this, you must relax the area of the inguinal crease, or kwa, as it is known in martial arts.

Another aspect of getting your footwork correct is repetition. If you know exactly where your feet should go and that you are going to put them in that position without thinking about it, you are mastering your footwork!

For Clockwise Stepping

1. Bend your knees and sink onto your kwa.

2. Sink your weight onto your right leg and step out with your left leg, turning your toes slightly inward.

3. Shift your weight onto your left foot and draw your right foot level with it.

4. Transfer your weight onto your right foot. Step out again with your left foot, as in step 2.

5. Take another step by repeating steps 4 and 5.

If you continue stepping like this, you will be walking the circle. Stepping forward is done with the outer (more yang) leg, with the inner (more yin) leg being drawn up to it. To step in a counterclockwise circle, simply reverse left and right when performing the steps. It is good to train for equal amounts of time in the clockwise and counterclockwise directions because this will prevent your training from developing one side of your body more than the other.

The Eight Fixed Postures of Ba Gua

As discussed earlier, the postures will change as you are walking the circle when your skill level is high enough. It is also possible to change your direction from clockwise to counterclockwise using a movement called palm change. The palm changes can be single- or double-handed and are an intrinsic part of the training. It is beyond the scope of this book to try to explain the subtleties of moving hand positions and palm changes.

We can, however, look at the fixed positions of ba gua. These positions can be held while you are walking the circle. This training opens the energy meridians of your body and allows the chi to flow. It is also good for strength training and balance. Start by learning how to walk the circle and work your way through holding each of the positions in a static way as you perform the exercise.

Press Down

Push your hands out in front of you, with your fingers pointing toward each other. Keep your arms soft and do not lock your elbows. The feeling in your arms should be the same as for the unbreakable arm (pages 96 to 97) in this and all other ba gua arm positions. Imagine that you are pressing energy away.

Embrace

Imagine that you are holding a small baby with your inner arm and are making a protective "fender" with your outer arm. This is actually the ward-off movement protecting your inner and outer circles.

Push Forward

Your arms are making a broken circle and your fingers are tilted so that they are pointing toward each other. Remember to keep your elbows soft! The energy is being pushed away from you, so imagine your energy projecting outward as you push.

Hold up the Heavens

This is similar to the standing-like-a-tree exercises that we looked at earlier. Open your arms and imagine that you are holding up the sky. Project your energy outward, in all directions.

Lion Plays Ball

Grabbing a ball, throwing it over the top of your head, and catching it with your other hand are similar to the feeling of this posture. One arm should be over your head and the other one should be extended.

Push Front and Back

Press one hand forward at about shoulder height and the other back, at about waist height. You should project with both hands as though you were trying to open sliding doors that you are stuck between.

Join Heaven and Earth

Raise one hand and point your fingers upward. Imagine that you are connecting with the heavens. The other hand should cross your body and extend toward the earth. You are making a connection between heaven and earth. In many mystical traditions, humans are the link between heaven and earth. You are symbolizing that link with this posture.

Dragon Turns Its Waist

Press your arms toward the center of your circle. Your inner arm should press toward the center of your rotational path, and your outer arm should cross your body before doing the same.

Other Tai Chi Moves

The movements shown so far are by no means definitive of the tai chi repertoire. When you consider that each of the five major styles of tai chi has literally hundreds of different movements, you can see that it would be impossible to cover them all. What follows is a sampler of some movements that are common throughout many tai chi styles, with an emphasis on the Yang style.

Tai Chi Kicks

Kicks are common in most martial styles, and tai chi is no exception. There are some subtle differences in the way that they are executed when compared to other styles, however. In tai chi and other internal styles, it is important to keep your back straight when you kick. This is different to the front kick in tae kwon do and karate, where the back arches to push the kick through, producing the powerful kick that you see experts use to break boards.

In tai chi, the back does not arch. This usually means that the kick will be lower. The emphasis with the tai chi kick is on stability. Try the following practice drills for kicking.

Heel Kick

1. Start in a bow stance, with your forearms crossed and your left leg leading.

2. Open your arms as you sink your weight onto your leading, left leg.

3. After your arms have opened, there should be no weight on your right leg. This frees you to lift your right knee as high as you can without bending your back.

4. Turn your body to your right. Push your right heel out for the heel kick.

5. Place your right leg in front of you in a bow stance and cross your forearms in front of your chest.

Instep Kick

1. Start in the empty stance, with your right leg behind you.

2. Open the toes of your left foot and raise your right hand.

3. Shift your weight onto your left foot.

4. Kick through with your right leg. As your foot travels forward, your right hand travels forward, too.

5. If you can kick high enough, the palm of your right hand can strike the instep of your right foot. When you raise your leg for the kick, lift your knee first.

6. Put your right foot down in front of you so that you are in the empty stance, with your weight on your left leg.

Repeat the kick using your left leg, following the same routine.

Lotus Kick

1. Start in the empty stance, with your weight on your right leg.

2. Shift your weight onto your left leg and then raise your right leg.

3. Kick by lifting your right knee first and then swinging your foot around in an arc. If you are supple enough, your right hand can tap the edge of your right foot at the maximum point of its swing.

Additional Moves

The following movements are useful to help you to understand some of the methodologies of tai chi. Both of the movements are taken from the Yang-style form.

Needle at the Sea Bottom

This is taken from the second section of the form. It looks quite easy, but is deceptively demanding on your body, and you must remember to keep your back straight. When you are standing straight, it is easy to lean one way or the other. The difficulty is increased if you are trying to bend your body forward, as in this move. The secret here is to be honest with yourself: if you cannot bend very far, wait until you develop the strength to do so.

1. Start in the brush-and-push posture (see page 140), with your right hand positioned in front of you.

2. Sink your weight onto your left leg and release your right leg. Let your right leg move forward.

3. Shift your weight onto your right leg as you relax the fingers of your right hand and raise your left hand.

4. Sink down onto your right leg. As you sink, simultaneously adjust your left foot for an empty stance and push forward with the fingertips of both hands.

You are now in the needle-at-the-sea-bottom posture. If you can keep your back straight, you will find that it is an excellent standing position if you want to work your legs seriously!

Snake Creeps Down

This move uses the drop stance (see page 78), and is another exercise that people can get wrong by trying to do too much. If you cannot drop your body without leaning your torso, simply do not drop as far.

1. Start in the single-whip posture (see pages 136 to 137).

2. Push your weight forward onto your left leg so that there is no weight on your right leg.

3. Twist your right foot through a right angle (or thereabouts) and simultaneously relax your left-hand fingertips, pointing them forward.

4. Drop your weight onto your right leg and pull back your left elbow.

5. Push from your right leg to drive your left-hand fingertips forward.

Martial Applications

Tai chi movements can be used for self-defense. This chapter also introduces you to martial applications, practice drills, pushing-hands exercises, and freestyle tai chi, all of which you can work on with a partner.

Self-defense in Tai Chi

Like any other martial arts system, tai chi has a number of movements that can be applied specifically to self-defense. The applications tend to be simple because if you actually need to defend yourself, it is likely to be against an aggressor who is quite dangerous. You are also going to be frightened, and when you are frightened, you forget things.

If a person attacks you, your aggressor probably thinks that he or she will win easily. The chances are that he or she will also be bigger than you, and this brings us to the first line of self-defense: a strong spirit. In tai chi, the way to stop an attack is not to be there when it happens. This applies very much to the spiritual aspect of tai chi. If you have a certain presence that suggests to a potential assailant that you have inner reserves, he or she may not attack you, but may go in search of a weaker victim instead. A strong presence and spirit will ward off most attackers.

If you cannot avoid such a situation, the following techniques may help. These concentrate mainly on escapes from grabs and holds. Other forms of attack are covered in the section on tai chi applications (see pages 187 to 200).

Escape from a Two-handed Grab to the Wrists

1. Imagine a scenario in which your attacker is trying to immobilize you by grabbing both of your wrists. Turn and look into the face of your opponent.

2. Point your fingertips downward.

3. Bend your wrists so that your palms are roughly parallel with the floor.

4. Push forward with your fingers as you exhale. Imagine that your fingertips are piercing your attacker's abdominal area.

5. Throw!

If you make the technique work, you will slip out of the attacker's grip on your wrists. If you manage to take the attacker by surprise, you could actually send him or her flying backward. If you are having difficulty, it could mean that you are trying to raise your hands instead of pushing them outward.

This is the opening form for nearly all tai chi sequences. Think about that. If all sequences use this movement, then there must be a reason for it.

Escape from a Single-handed Grab: No. 1

This is a simplified version of needle at the sea bottom (see page 175), and a useful technique if your attacker grabs your right hand with his or her right hand, that is, with the two hands crossing in front of you. Be very careful when practicing this technique. If you are overenthusiastic with your training partner, you could easily damage his or her wrist. If you use the technique very powerfully and suddenly, you will either break or dislocate the attacker's wrist. If it is not working properly, make sure that you are not tilting the hand when you point your fingers at the attacker's abdomen.

1. Your attacker grabs your wrist.

2. Trap the attacker's hand by placing your other hand on top of it.

3. Turn the wrist that you are holding toward your body slightly. Extend your fingers.

4. Bring your fingers over the top of your attacker's wrist and point your fingertips at his or her abdomen. This will put your attacker into a powerful wristlock.

Escape from a Single-handed Grab: No. 2

If your attacker grabs you with the other hand, the needle-at-the-sea-bottom technique can still work, but the following technique, taken from apparent close-up (see page 146), is probably easier.

1. Your attacker grabs your right hand with his or her left hand.

2. Rotate your right forearm and push it forward slightly. Place your left hand somewhere underneath your elbow.

3. Pull back your right elbow as you swing out with your left forearm.

4. This will entangle your attacker.

The secret to getting this movement correct is the turning of the forearm in step 2. It is difficult for the attacker to stop you from doing this, and it breaks their grip. After that, it is simply a matter of coordinating the movement of the two arms.

Escape from a Shoulder Grab

This move works best if the attacker has grabbed a good handful of your clothing.

1. Your attacker grabs your shoulder.

2. Put your hand on top of his or her hand.

3. Make a big circle with your elbow and then cut downward with your elbow.

4. This will be sufficient to ensure that you escape the attacker's grip.

If you want to go a little farther, you are set to put your opponent into a shoulder lock, but be careful if you are just practicing. This movement is fundamental to the tai chi style and occurs in all actions in which the elbow moves downward.

Escape from a Bear Hug

There are hundreds of escapes from this type of attack across the martial arts styles. This movement is very simple, but, with practice, is also very effective.

1. You are grabbed from behind.

2. Open your armpits to make a small ward-off movement with both arms.

3. Suddenly twist your body. Your partner's grip will be broken.

4. Continue to twist, and you will throw your partner.

Tai Chi Applications

All tai chi movements have a series of martial applications, and these are integral to tai chi as a whole.

If you learn one application of a movement, try to use it as your starting point to work out others. The following application sequence is the most important in the Yang style of tai chi. If you do not understand this sequence, you do not understand tai chi.

Grasping the Sparrow's Tail

Before you start, remember the eight energies of tai chi. The first four are ward off, roll back, press, and push. They are considered the most important of the energies because the remaining four energies derive from them. They also happen to be the first four moves of grasping the sparrow's tail, and it is for this reason that this movement is repeated many times throughout the sequence.

The movement has four parts, as described on the following pages.

Ward Off

Here you intercept the attack using a ward-off movement and then use ward off to control.

1. Stand opposite your partner.

2. Your partner throws a punch with his or her left hand. Intercept it by cutting upward with the fingertips of your left hand.

3. Step forward into the bow stance. As you step, simultaneously wrap your left forearm around your partner's punching arm.

If you were to apply this move suddenly, it could do serious damage to your partner's arm, so be careful. Another, less damaging, way to control is to push forward slightly. This upsets your partner's center of gravity and shoulders and makes it very difficult for him or her to throw a punch with the other hand.

4. As your weight sinks onto your left leg, catch your partner's wrist with your right hand.

Roll Back

In roll back, you draw an attack inward and use the leverage of your partner's arm to control.

1. Your partner punches with his or her right fist.

2. The best way to stop somebody from hitting you is to get out of the way. Use the bow stance to step forward and simultaneously catch your partner's wrist and elbow.

3. As with ward off, the sudden and powerful application of this technique can be seriously damaging. Once you have your partner in the roll-back position, it is nearly impossible for him or her to hit you with any force.

Press

This application shows press as an attacking technique. Your right arm is passive, with the motor force coming from your left arm. You could use the movement either to push your partner away or, if you wanted to do some damage, you could apply the technique with explosive force, known as fa jing. When applied in this way, the technique can cause serious damage to internal organs.

1. Stand in the press position. Shift onto your back leg and let your partner push your forearm back.

2. A sudden application of force (fa jing) will throw your partner.

After a little practice, you will be able to push your partner away quite easily.

Push

With this movement, you do not just simply push your arms out: there is also an upward motion, which undermines your partner's center of gravity.

Shift back in the bow stance, with your hands ready for the press position. Try to push your arms straight out.

If you are stronger than your partner, you will succeed, but that is not really tai chi! Let's try again!

1. Place your hands against your partner.

2. Expand your body, pushing upward from the floor to throw your partner.

As with the press movement, the push could be used to give you some room. If you are a good kicker, you could use the technique to give you the space in which to kick. An alternative is to use the explosive fa-jing force to send your opponent flying.

Waving Hands Like Clouds

Waving hands like clouds appears in one version or another in all of the tai chi forms, and is characteristic of the strategies used in tai chi. In particular, it uses a soft contact to redirect an attack and then follows with an attack.

1. Your partner punches with his or her left fist. Intercept it with your right hand.

2. Turn your waist and arms to redirect the attack.

3. By this time, you have done the main job: stopping yourself from being hit! If you want to reward your attacker for his or her trouble, suddenly sink your weight as you lift the attacker's left arm. Depending on how you use this technique, it could be used to damage or control the arm.

Brush and Push

In brush and push, we have a defense that is immediately returned with an attack. The defense and attack should be properly timed for maximum effect.

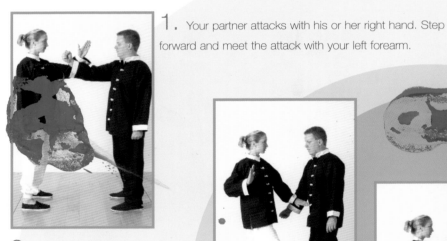

1. Your partner attacks with his or her right hand. Step forward and meet the attack with your left forearm.

2. As your weight transfers forward into the bow stance, drive your left forearm downward in a spiral and prepare to push with your right hand.

3. Finish by pressing down with your left hand and attacking with your right hand.

If you were to imagine this technique without the attack, it would still work as a deflection, and would probably put your opponent or partner off-balance. The problem here is that the direction in which he or she would fall would be on to you. The counterattack prevents this from happening.

Strum the Lute

Strum the lute uses pull-down energy. This move was a favorite of Sun Lu Tang (see pages 48 to 49) and features prominently in his form. The version shown here is from the first section of Yang-style tai chi.

1. Your partner attacks with his or her right hand.

2. Use your right hand to deflect the attack.

3. Shift into the empty stance as you push upward with the fingertips of your left hand. This will put your partner in an arm lock that can damage the elbow if you are not careful.

Raise Hands and White Crane
Spreads Its Wings

This sequence from the Yang-style tai chi routine shows how one movement can naturally flow into another, so that you can immediately follow on with a suitable technique if the previous one failed.

For this to work, you will need to have a very clear understanding of the techniques.

Raise Hands

1. Your partner attacks with his or her right hand.

2. Step into the empty stance and attack" his or her wrist and elbow.

If you got this move right, it could break the elbow. However, we are assuming that you need to continue.

Shoulder Stroke

1. Rotate your arms as you press down. The power in this movement comes from sinking farther into the empty stance. This can be used to control or break the elbow.

2. Step forward and simultaneously strike your opponent's body with your body and his or her face with your right hand.

You have hit the attacker with a series of attacks. Now just push him or her away.

White Crane Spreads Its Wings

Push all of your weight down onto your left leg as your body spirals upward into the empty stance. Perform a ward off with your left arm and counterbalance this by pushing down with your right hand.

Parting the Wild Horse's Mane

This technique is a good example of splitting energy. Differential pressure from your legs makes your waist turn so that you can throw out your arms very powerfully.

1. Your partner attacks with his or her left fist.

2. You deflect with your left hand while turning your body to avoid the strike.

3. Step forward into a bow stance (you will have to get close for this one).

4. Pull down with your left hand as you uncoil your right arm. Hit the attacker with your shoulder, elbow, and then forearm. This will usually send the attacker tumbling over your leg.

Another way to use the same technique is to perform the uncoiling motion as a strike with either the outer edge of your forearm or the edge of your hand, as shown on the left.

Heel Kick

The heel kick is very powerful, and can be quick if performed correctly. It is useful for getting under an attacker's guard, and if you are confident in your kicks, it makes a very good self-defense movement.

1. Your attacker throws a punch.

2. As always, your defense is to get out of the way. Do this by stepping into the bow stance. As you step, cross your arms in front of your body.

3. Open your arms to redirect the punch and expose the attacker's vulnerable ribs.

4. Lift your knee and kick into the area of the floating rib.

If you cannot kick very high, you can still kick with power. If your kick hits anywhere along your attacker's side, it will certainly slow him or her down!

Instep Kick

The instep kick is powerful and can be performed quickly, taking your opponent by surprise—very useful in self-defense!

1. Your attacker reaches out to grab you around your neck.

2. Block his hands with your right hand, raising your left hand to protect your neck.

3. Deliver a sharp kick with your right leg. This should finish the attack!

Lotus Kick

In tai chi, we are always playing with opposites, and the lotus kick is a good example of this.

When practicing the kick, it is desirable, although not vital, to make the kick as high as you can because it can be used to strike the side of a person's head.

What, then, is the lotus kick used for? Apart from looking good (which it always does when executed correctly), it has applications that are more like tai chi than a kick to the head.

1. Your partner attacks.

2. Sidestep your partner's attack in the empty stance.

3. Sweep low with your leg and push across with your arms.

4. Follow through with the kick.

5. This will knock your partner to the floor (warning: do not actually knock your partner to the floor unless he or she is used to breaking falls and you are training on mats).

Be a sport and give your partner a hand up!

Tai Chi Practice Drills

When you started to learn self-defense and the martial applications, you made the transition from solo practice to practicing with a partner. If you have tried some of the examples, you will have found that practicing with a partner gives a whole new dimension to your tai chi.

You are not expected to instantly be able to apply all of the tai chi applications to two-person practice. First, you must learn the applications, then you must train with them. Various practice drills have been devised to help you. Usually, they involve a cyclical pattern of movement. This means that you can practice continually and work with the movement.

Grasping the Sparrow's Tail

This is the most difficult of the practice drills. If you can manage this, you can certainly manage the following exercises. If, for some reason, you find it difficult, try the others first and then come back to it.

1. Stand opposite your partner. Your partner throws a punch with his or her left fist . . .

2. . . . and you deflect it . . .

3. . . . with your right hand.

4. Step into the first position ward off and lock your partner's elbow.

5. Your partner tries to escape by lifting his or her elbow. Do not try to stop him or her, but go with the flow.

6. Turn your waist and move into the roll-back position.

9. Prepare for press to return the attack.

8. Your partner tries to escape by elbowing toward your abdomen.

7. The roll-back position.

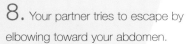

10. Press toward your partner.

11. Your partner deflects the press with an upward block.

12. Your partner sees an opening and prepares to punch with his or her right hand.

13. The punch is thrown.

14. Use your partner's forearm to block the punch.

15. Push your partner with both hands.

16. Step forward as you push. Your partner absorbs the push by stepping back.

17. Now your partner will deflect your right hand.

18. Your turn to be caught in ward off!

Repeat the sequence, reversing the roles.

Punch

This one is fun to practice blindfolded, but make sure that you can do it with your eyes open first. It teaches you how to "stick" to your opponent. If you can develop the sensitivity to feel, rather than see, what is going on, then you will learn new levels of tai chi.

1. Your partner punches with his or her right fist.

2. You block the punch with your forearm.

3. This gives you an opening for a punch, so you take it.

4. Your partner "sticks" to your forearm and uses this to block your attack.

5. Now it is your partner's turn to punch again.

6. Do not lose contact. You can block in the same way, preparing for the next punch.

Waving Hands Like Clouds (Single-handed)

If you want, you can sidestep in this movement once you have mastered the fixed step shown here.

1. Stand opposite your partner. Touch your forearms together as shown.

2. Try to reach forward. As your partner feels your intent to move forward, he or she will deflect to one side.

3. From this new position for the arms, try to push forward again.

4. Your partner will stick to you and guide you away from his or her central line to deflect again to the other side.

5. Repeat the movement.

Note that the partners are not equal in this arrangement. One is attacking and the other is defending, even though it may look the same to the untrained eye. Train equally, switching between attacking and defending, so that you both have a turn doing each.

Brush and Push

1. Stand opposite your partner in the bow stance, with your left leg forward.

2. Your partner pushes toward you with his or her left hand.

3. Use your left forearm to block as you prepare to push with your right hand.

4. Push with your right hand.

5. This time, your partner will block with his or her right hand and prepare to strike with the left hand.

6. Keep contact with your partner and deflect the push as you prepare for your next push.

Repeat the sequence.

When you become accustomed to the practice, you can change legs while practicing or step backward as your partner advances. With this technique, an inequality arises from the fact that you are blocking with the same hand and pushing with the same hand all of the time. Try changing the attacking arm to equalize the practice.

Knees

In martial arts, it is common to distract an opponent by making him or her think that you are going to attack high to the face, when you are actually attacking low to the legs. The following routine is about learning how to upset a person's balance from below while maintaining your own balance. It is very simple, and excellent for taking people by surprise.

1. Stand opposite your partner in the bow stance. Your right shin should be touching your partner's right shin.

2. Push your knee forward, moving it in a circular pattern. If your partner is unprepared, this will undermine his or her balance and could topple him or her.

3. Your partner yields to your attack and replies with an exact copy of your move.

4. Repeat the sequence.

5. Remember that you should yield to your partner's attack.

You need to make a circular movement with your knees. If you do not, you will simply push against each other, causing one another injury.

Elbow

An elbow attack is a devastating martial arts technique. This routine uses the energies from grasping the sparrow's tail to practice the elbow strike.

1. Your partner attacks with his or her right elbow. Slow the attack with your left hand.

2. Redirect the attack with your right hand.

3. Press the attack out of the way with your left hand.

4. Return the attack with your right elbow.

5. Your partner then redirects your attack.

6. Press to get your elbow away.

7. You block the returning attack with your elbow. Continue the cycle.

With practice, it is possible to make the technique very fast. After a while, you may become so fast that observers will only see a blur where your arms are.

Tai Chi Pushing Hands

One of the most famous parts of the tai chi syllabus is pushing hands. This is the bridge between the tai chi form practice, the practice drills, and freestyle tai chi movement. You start by learning with one hand and then progress to pushing hands using both hands. Once you have mastered two-handed pushing hands, you can start to learn moving-step pushing hands.

These pushing-hands routines are in the form of set sequences. You perform a movement and your partner responds with an appropriate movement. There is a testing aspect here, too. If you are pushing hands with somebody and sense that he or she is off-balance, you can give a little push to allow him or her to feel that they are off-balance. One of the lessons in pushing hands is called investing in loss. The late tai chi master Chen Man Ching coined the phrase during the 1960s. It means that you can learn from practicing with a person who can push you. Eventually, you will learn how to avoid the push and push your partner instead. Your partner then has the same job: to stop you from pushing him or her. By investing in loss, you will both improve.

All of the pushing-hands movements should be done slowly and deliberately.

Try changing hands. All of the descriptions that follow are for the right hand as the dominant hand. Try the same routines with the left hand being dominant.

No. 1: Single-handed on a Horizontal Plane

This single-handed version of pushing hands simulates an attack like a push or a punch. Your yielding hand meets the attack. This redirects the force of the attack so that you can return the attack. Your partner follows with the same maneuver and the cycle continues.

2. Step forward with your right leg into the bow stance. Adjust your right foot to a 45-degree angle. Both partners should now make a ward-off posture with their right arms and touch their wrists together.

1. Stand opposite your partner.

3. Decide who will push first.

4. If your partner pushes first, allow your ward-off arm to become soft as you shift back and turn your waist. When you have reached your maximum position for yielding, most of your weight should be on your right leg. Remember to keep your back straight.

5. Push from the heel of your right foot.

6. Extend the push in your partner's direction. Now it is your partner's turn to yield. Your partner's yielding should be receptive to your push.

7. Do not start to yield until you feel the push from your partner.

8. Let the attack come to you as you yield.

No. 2: Single-handed on an Inclined Plane

This routine works in exactly the same way as the last one, except that the plane of movement is inclined. The application here would be to deflect a slapping attack to the face. The starting procedure is exactly the same as that of the last pushing-hands routine.

1. Stand opposite your partner. Step to the side with your left foot into the wu chi position (see page 73). Your feet should be shoulder-width apart.

2. Step forward with your right leg into the bow stance. Adjust your right foot to a 45-degree angle. Now both make a ward-off posture with your right arms, touching your wrists together.

3. Your partner should make an arc with his or her right hand as if to slap your face.

4. Shift back onto your left leg and deflect your partner's hand with your right hand.

5. Push from your right leg as though you were aiming a slap toward your partner's face.

6. As in the last example, your partner deflects your blow and returns with another.

No. 3: Single-handed on a Vertical Plane

This version of pushing hands deflects a finger thrust and retaliates with another finger thrust.

1. Stand opposite your partner. Step to the side with your left foot into the wu chi position. Your feet should be shoulder-width apart.

2. Step forward with your left leg into the bow stance. Adjust your right foot to a 45-degree angle. Both partners should now make a ward-off posture with their right arms and touch their wrists together.

3. Your partner thrusts toward your neck.

4. Turn your body and deflect the thrust with a downward motion.

5. This puts you in a position to be able to thrust at your partner's abdomen.

6. Your partner turns and deflects the thrust.

7. Your partner is again ready to thrust.

As well as alternating between the left and right hand, you should alternate between a high thrust and a lower thrust.

No. 4: Double-handed on a Horizontal Plane

This routine is a progression of the first sequence. If you can perform the single-handed pushing-hands exercise, you should have very little difficulty with the double-handed version. The trick with all of the double-handed versions of pushing hands is to allow the contact that you make with your passive hand to move. The contact will start on the elbow, but will slide up and down. As with the single-handed versions, you should try alternating your leading leg so that you practice with both sides of your body.

1. Stand opposite your partner. Step to the side with your left foot into the wu chi position. Your feet should be shoulder-width apart.

2. Step forward with your left leg into the bow stance. Adjust your right foot to a 45-degree angle. Both of you should now make a ward-off posture with your right arms, touching your wrists together.

3. Place your left hand on your partner's right elbow. Your partner should do the same.

4. Your partner now pushes with both hands.

5. Use the ward off from your right arm to redirect the push and shift back. As your partner pushes against your wrist and elbow, allow your contact hand to slide up and down your partner's forearm. Shift back onto your right leg and yield to the attack.

6. It is now your turn to push. Prepare for the push by placing your left hand on your partner's elbow.

7. Push from your back heel toward your partner.

8. Your partner deflects the push in the same way that you just did and the cycle starts again.

Nos. 5 and 6

Once you have mastered the three versions
of the single-handed pushing hands and the
two-handed version that follows (no. 4), the
rest are very simple to understand. They
follow exactly the same procedure as the
last sequence. To make life easy, start by
doing the single-handed exercises shown in
numbers 2 and 3, and make them two-
handed (nos. 5 and 6) by placing your
other hand on your partner's elbow, as
shown here.

Number 5.

Number 6.

Freestyle Tai Chi

The pictures below and on the next page show examples of freestyle tai chi sparring. The important aspect that sets freestyle tai chi sparring apart from other martial styles is the use of yielding. The movements may not look exactly the same as in the form practice or pushing hands, but the principles of tai chi should be adhered to. It is important not to rush into freestyle sparring in tai chi because this often results in messy sparring bouts that bear no resemblance to tai chi.

A.

1. The punch is deflected.

2. Fold the elbow.

3. Turn the body for roll back.

B.

1. Deflect the push with press.

2. A rising block is made in preparation to punch.

3. Too late!

What Happens Next?

Learning tai chi is a process of continual education. Developing a strategy for your own learning will both enhance the effect and speed up the process.

Improving Your Tai Chi

In tai chi, there are several schools of thought as to how to improve your technique. One way is to learn more than one style, and this approach can be useful if you are trying to widen your knowledge of the martial arts. This is also a good approach if you are looking for many different applications. However, in the world of martial arts, there is also an understanding that the person who has worked on one technique for a year will be more dangerous than the person who has studied many techniques over the same period of time.

The same logic is also true of movements within the form that you are learning. It is not through laziness that the Yang family included grasping the sparrow's tail at every opportunity, but to encourage the Yang-style tai chi student to practice that move over and over again. It teaches the four primary energies in tai chi. Even if grasping the sparrow's tail were the only part of the form that you knew, but you could perform it perfectly, you would have a profound knowledge of tai chi.

In tai chi, you need to be patient with yourself. It may seem as though your instructor is holding you back by making you practice the same movement all of the time, but this is how you will improve.

An instructor will help to correct your moves.

The Ten Essences

You are serious about learning tai chi. You do not mind putting in the work—in fact, you are looking forward to it. You have joined a class and have started to learn one of the tai chi forms. What happens next? This is where effort comes in.

In the old days of China, putting the effort in, if you were a martial artist, was unquestioned. If you were a professional bodyguard or soldier, as many martial artists were, you would often find yourself in a life-or-death situation. Without the training, you were likely to be killed quite quickly. Nowadays, thankfully, we do not need to train for our lives. However, this removes one obvious motivating factor in training. Coupled with the fact that most people work and have a family to look after, it is a wonder that this art survives at all.

The secret is to train intelligently. You need to ensure that every part of your practice is significant, and that you are being as efficient as possible with your time. To assist with this, there are various formulas that have been handed down through the ages, among them the ten essences of tai chi.

Although these essences have been around since the days of Yang Chen Fu, they have been arranged into the natural sequence described here by Christopher Pei. They encapsulate most of the other formulas that have been devised over the years to help students to learn tai chi.

The Ten Essences

1. Lift the head to raise the spirit.
2. Sink the shoulders and lower the elbows.
3. Loosen the chest and round the back.
4. Loosen the waist.
5. Separate the substantial and the insubstantial.
6. Coordinate the upper and lower body.
7. Continuous movement.
8. Unite the internal intent with the body.
9. Use the mind, not force.
10. Seek stillness in motion and motion within stillness.

Write the ten essences down on a piece of paper and keep it with you at all times. Learn the essences until you can repeat them in the correct sequence. This is like learning a poem. If you can learn it by heart, then you can think about the meanings of the words and what they mean to your tai chi and many other activities.

No. 1: Lift the Head to Raise the Spirit

This is probably the simplest to understand and the easiest to forget. If you imagine two people, one in high spirits and the other low, you can immediately see who is showing the strongest spirit of the two.

Keeping the body upright is a sign of a strong spirit.

The message is a two-way signal. If your spirits are low, try lifting your head. You may find that you start to feel better in yourself. In the tai chi form, we develop this in many ways, and should pay attention to the position of our heads and necks. As soon as you become tired or start to forget, your head can sag and your tai chi loses its spirit.

No. 2: Sink the Shoulders and Lower the Elbows

Try standing for a while with your shoulders raised up near your ears and take note of the effort that it takes to keep them in that high position. Unless your shoulders are very relaxed, you waste energy by keeping them higher than they need to be. Also, lowering your shoulders lowers your center of gravity, which makes you physically more stable and therefore also emotionally.

We can elevate our shoulders for many reasons. A common one is emotional. Think about what happens when you see somebody hit another person's head. As a protective reflex, the shoulders will usually rise. If your history is such that you feel that you have been physically or emotionally "hit around the head," it is possible for this to affect your shoulders. Frequently, in such cases, when people learn to loosen their shoulders, there can be a tremendous sense of emotional freedom, which can be very positive for the person's emotional well-being.

In a martial arts sense, if your shoulders are raised, then your elbows will also be raised, which makes it easy for a person to trap your elbow.

See how much more relaxed you look if your shoulders are not tense.

No. 3: Loosen the Chest and Round the Back

Try the following experiment.

Breathing

Part 1: stand at attention. Pull your shoulders back and push out your chest. Now try to take a long, deep breath. Note how comfortable or uncomfortable it feels, and feel how much breath you can take in.

Part 2: stand in the wu chi position. Relax your body and round your shoulders very slightly so that you can just feel the muscles in your back open and the front of your chest feels soft. Take another deep breath. Note the same things—the length of the breath and how comfortable it feels.

Which resulted in the longest breath and felt the most comfortable? Most people agree that standing at attention restricts the breath and is uncomfortable. The third essence suggests that you loosen the chest and round the back. This is the opposite of standing at attention, when the chest is tight and the back loose.

Many people have a habit of breathing with the upper chest only. If you sink your breath into your abdomen and relax your chest, you will normally find that your breathing becomes deeper and that you breathe more efficiently. This also implies a way of moving your body. If you move your arm to a position that makes your chest feel tight, the muscles in your back cannot be used and you lose power. This is all connected with the third essence.

No. 4: Loosen the Waist

The first three essences were all connected with the upper body. It is useful to work on them in the sequence given because this helps you to fit your body into the rules of tai chi. If you master the first three essences, you will walk upright (essence one), relax your shoulders (essence two), and use abdominal breathing (essence three).

Now think about your center of gravity. If you lean forward or backward, your center of gravity moves. If you raise your shoulders, your center of gravity rises.

The waist has not rotated, so the movement looks, and feels, awkward.

If the waist turns, the movement is softer.

When you apply the first three essences, your center of gravity becomes lower through a natural process. This allows your waist to move more freely because your inner, core muscles are stabilizing your body in a more efficient way.

When your center of gravity comes to a position just below your navel, called the tan tien, the energy in the waist can move more freely. This is the fourth essence, loosen the waist.

No. 5: Separate the Substantial and the Insubstantial

Imagine trying to drive an automobile with a heavy roof rack. The handling of the vehicle would be different from normal because of its high center of gravity. If the center of gravity is in an optimum position, the handling is better and the vehicle is easier to control. How does this apply to tai chi?

It concentrates on smooth delivery. If you wobble, you cannot regulate the flow of power in a skillful way. In tai chi, as in many other martial arts and sports, the strength of the arms derives from that of the legs.

Imagine a rock climber. If he or she is beyond novice level, the arms are vital, but

The push starts from the back heel and moves like a wave through the body.

all of the motive force comes from the legs. In order to move one foot, all of the body's weight must be carried by the other foot while a foothold is being found.

Tai chi is exactly the same. In a push, all of the weight starts on the back leg. In the language of the ten essences, the leg has become "substantial," that is, it carries all of the weight. As you apply the push, your back leg straightens and drives your arms forward. Your weight transfers from the back leg to the front leg, so the front leg becomes more substantial. This can only be achieved when your frame is stable enough to allow the center of gravity to drop to the tan tien and you can control the delivery of power in your legs.

No. 6: Coordinate the Upper and Lower Body

The first five essences set your physical frame for tai chi, while essences six to ten teach you how to use that frame, much of which has to do with the coordination of the body and mind. Look at the pictures above right and see which ones you think have upper- and lower-body coordination.

In picture 1, the legs have completed the move before the hands. You can see this from the fact that the legs are in the finishing position for the bow stance, but the arms have not straightened out for the push. In picture 2, the arms reach maximum extension at the same time that the legs

finish. This is powerful because the whole body is being used for the movement.

Now try again with roll back. In picture 3, the arms have finished making the roll back, but the legs are still changing. In picture 4, you can see that the person has shifted back in the roll-back position at the same time as the arms complete the move. The understanding of these essences is quite subtle, but if you can grasp their meaning, your tai chi will never be the same again!

No. 7: Continuous Movement

Think for a while about the previous essence, coordinating the upper and lower body. If the arm completes the move before the leg, the arm has to wait for the leg to catch up before it can perform the next movement. Clearly, this indicates a problem with upper- and lower-body coordination.

If the movements are smooth and continuous, then the upper and lower body must be in time with each other. In this way, this essence—continuous movement—can only happen once you have coordinated the upper and lower body. If the upper and lower body are working together, you will have the seventh essence.

The sixth and seventh essences of tai chi rule the coordination of the upper and lower body. Once you start to have a feel for the sixth essence and your arms and legs are working together, you can refine it further by checking that there are no halts in your movement.

No. 8: Unite the Internal Intent with the Body

The previous two essences, six and seven, help the upper and lower body to work as one. In the next two, the mind becomes the focus. Until now, you have been learning how to get your frame right and then how to move with your frame. Early on, you learned the exercise that helps you to understand how strong a relaxed body can be: the unbreakable-arm exercise (see pages 96 to 98). When you reach this level of tai chi, this understanding is applied to all movements.

When you push, you imagine that your energy expands with your body. When you withdraw, you imagine that your energy contracts with your body. This is the motion of yin and yang applied to the form. The

movements extend past your body, at least in your imagination. This makes you push through a target.

When you have united the intent of your mind with the motions of your body, it means that you are very conscious of your actions. You cannot achieve this balance if your mind is constantly wandering off to other subjects. Mastering the eighth essence means that your body and mind are constantly flowing together in the tai chi form, and that your mind is entirely with you in your actions.

No. 9: Use the Mind, Not Force

Mastering the ninth essence is similar to mastering the seventh. You cannot manage it until you have understood the preceding essence. A good example of the ninth essence is in the use of pushing hands. When you are just using your body, pushing hands can be physically hard. When you start to understand the power that comes from linking your body

and mind, however, you no longer need to use physical force, but instead follow your partner's energy and apply your energy when the time is right.

In this way, your tai chi has progressed from pushing your partner to a flow of yin and yang between you and your partner. This is an advanced stage of tai chi.

No. 10: Seek Stillness in Motion and Motion Within Stillness

The tenth essence is the essence of the artist. To get an idea of this, go to a concert at which you know a virtuoso musician is performing. As the musician plays the notes, he or she is not thinking about the notes and scales. Most people who reach this stage talk about feeling that the world around them has stopped and that they are completely in the moment.

This feeling of being in the moment allows the virtuoso to create masterpieces that seem impossible to the lesser player. The difference is that, one way or another, the virtuoso has managed to pass through the stages of learning a skill to the point where the skill just happens and the art flows through him or her.

Other Sources of Information

Masters of tai chi were teaching students the art long before the ten essences were thought of, and some very proficient modern masters may never even have heard of them. However, if you take a look at the writings of the masters, it is possible to find a strong correlation between what they have written and the ten essences. As an example, look at *Body Principles*, an instructional note by Wu-Yu-Hsiang (1812–1880).

A line-by-line examination of this work offers the following observations.

Relax the chest; raise the back. If you look at essence number three, loosen the chest and round the back, you will see the same instructions.

Enclose the solar plexus. Essence number three again. Enclosing the solar plexus is a way of asking a student to not force the chest outward.

Protect the cheekbones. This means that you should keep your chin pointing downward so that your cheeks do not protrude. This is not just to stop them from being hit, but opens the back of your neck and stretches your spine, as in the first essence: lift the head to raise the spirit.

Lift the head. This is essence number one again.

Suspend the solar plexus. There is a saying in tai chi that your body should be as though it were being suspended from a cord at the crown of your head. The idea is that you lift your head and all other parts of your body feel as though they are hanging from a central location. This is another way of expressing the first essence.

Loosen the shoulders. Look at essence number two, sink the shoulders and lower the elbows.

Wu-Yu-Hsiang writes:

Relax the chest.
Raise the back.
Enclose the solar plexus.
Protect the cheekbones.
Lift the head.
Suspend the solar plexus.
Loosen the shoulders.
Sink the elbows.
Be evasive.
Avoid conflict.

Sink the elbows. This is essence number two again.

Be evasive. In tai chi, we do not meet a force head on because the strongest force will always win. Instead, we move around the force. This is a strategic aspect of tai chi that works through uniting intent with the body, essence number eight.

Avoid conflict. Always a good idea! If somebody throws a punch, the best thing to do is not to be there. This applies in the martial situation; it is the idea of stepping out of the energy of an attack rather than trying to meet it head on. The eighth essence is the closest expression to this.

As you can see, some of the words are even the same. This is not surprising because the information comes from the *Yang Family Tai Chi Classics*, which Yang Cheng Fu would definitely have seen.

Using the I-Ching

If you are hunting for different ways of looking at your tai chi, the I-Ching can usually provide some sort of inspiration. You do not need to learn how to use the book as a divining tool to gain from its knowledge. Reading the meanings of the hexagrams and their relationship to one another can provide illuminating insights.

For example, in tai chi, we need to study the interaction of yin and yang. In the I-Ching, we study the same thing. The first hexagram is chien, the creative. It is completely yang, represented by expansion and movement. Its essence is in power or energy. Time is implied within this hexagram because it would be impossible to expand without time. Without time, there can be no movement.

The next hexagram is kun, the receptive. Kun represents the yielding power of yin. It is the female counterpart of the male principle of chien. Kun cannot be regarded as a separate entity to chien because it represents space. Without space, there can be no movement, and without movement, there is no energy.

From the I-Ching, we gain an idea of the inseparability of yin and yang. Without yin, there can be no yang and vice versa. In our tai chi forms, we cannot have yang movements followed by more yang movements. We need to withdraw and become yin before we can become yang again. Yin and yang must therefore form a cycle, flowing around each other.

Cross-training

Most modern tai chi teachers recognize the fact that cross-training in different disciplines will help your tai chi. When starting out, it is probably best to avoid other styles of martial art, however, because it is easy to confuse them.

In the martial schools of China and Japan, horseback-riding and archery were encouraged. The idea was that horseback-riding would teach you to keep an upright posture and direct movement from your waist, archery improving your hand–eye coordination.

Think about the kind of cross-training that would suit you. Do you need to become more supple? Try yoga. Do you get out of breath in your form? Try an aerobic exercise like running or playing football.

Just about any activity can be regarded as cross-training. When I play the guitar, I try to use it as an exercise in being mindful of the moment, rather like a meditation, which feeds straight back into the tenth essence.

Skill Levels in Tai Chi

In tai chi, just as in any other art, there are various levels of skill. If you want to train intelligently, you will need some idea as to what your skill level is.

This can be a very subjective matter. In such styles as tae kwon do and karate, there is a defined grading system. The color of your belt tells you where you are with your training. There is no equivalent grading system in tai chi.

A good reason for this is that tai chi is not entirely a martial style. Gradings usually indicate your ability on the sparring mats. If you are a black belt in tae kwon do, then a black belt in karate should be fairly closely matched in terms of fighting skill. If you have been training in tai chi for the same amount of time as the black belts in tae kwon do and karate, you will have reached a high skill level. This does not necessarily mean that you would be their equal on the sparring mats, however.

In tai chi, free sparring does not normally occur until quite an advanced stage (see page 242). We do, however, develop other areas, such as that of chi, which are not touched on in the other arts until quite late on. In the end, the result is similar. All martial artists will work on the "spirit": the arts are all different paths up the same mountain.

Self-assessment and continual learning can improve your skill level.

The only way for tai chi practitioners to test their skill is by looking inward and being honest in their self-assessment. You can use the ten essences as a kind of reference here. To begin with the first essence and progress to the last in the correct sequence is a journey. If you see a person training with his or her eyes on the floor most of the time, the first essence is clearly not in place. It does not matter if the person has been training for many years; if the first essence is not in place, the other essences cannot be either.

Are the shoulders relaxed? Is the chest soft? Is the waist moving freely? Does the person know where his or her weight should be? Are the hands and feet coordinated and moving smoothly? Does the person look as

though he or she is using intent? Is there energy flow? You will not be able to answer some of these questions until you have reached the level yourself. Used in this way, the ten essences can be a valuable guide to determining your skill level and that of others.

The Learning Program in Tai Chi

If you join a tai chi class, you will want to know what you are getting into. You are about to invest time and money in learning the art, so it is a good idea to find out what it involves. Here are a few pointers as to what might be included in a good learning program. It is not intended to be definitive: this is how I work and learn from my teachers, but this is not the only way.

First Level

At this level, a student will be trying to understand the tai chi body frame and how to move within that frame. This will usually involve exercises to loosen the body and mind. These can be flowing qi gong exercises and standing qi gong exercises. The student will learn how to integrate this knowledge into her tai chi form and may start some simple pushing-hands exercises.

Second Level

The student will have become comfortable with the form practice, and the pushing-hands movements are smooth and soft. The form may have been completed and the student will have moved on to two-handed pushing hands. The student will have a good understanding of yin and yang and knows how to express them with the body. As the student no longer needs to worry about the positioning of her hands and feet, she will start to feel the energy movement within them. The student starts to unlock the secrets of chi.

Third Level

At the third level, the student has an understanding of the eight energies in tai chi and of how to use them. She will start to work with more complex pushing-hands patterns and will probably begin to learn to use a weapon, such as the sword, the energies being easier to understand. This is a level where we learn to use intent and to move the chi.

Fourth Level

At the fourth level, the student is in control of the eight energies and no longer needs to worry about them. She is developing a continual feeling of the flow of chi. The tai chi saber form is a good way of learning this flow of chi because the techniques use many energies at the same time. The student will probably have started to learn moving-step pushing hands.

Fifth Level

At this level of training, the energy just flows and the student does not particularly need to work on it. The advanced student at this level has already gone through that stage. Students who have reached this level will be able to perform freestyle pushing hands with bare hands and weapons. This is a very high level of tai chi.

Finding a Teacher

The ultimate tai chi teacher understands all aspects of the art, including healing, martial arts, and energy, along with all of the side issues and philosophies that are attached to the art. The teacher should also be a person with whom you can get along and who can inspire you to reach new and higher goals.

Such teachers exist, but are rare. If your teacher is not the highest-level master in the world, you should not be put off training with him or her. No teacher can tell you everything. It may be that you have a teacher who is trying to get a point across to you and is not succeeding. If you learn that point from another source, the teacher should be able to acknowledge your success and help you to grow from it.

In Conclusion: Spirit

So what is the ultimate goal of tai chi training? That is actually quite an easy question to answer, and can be summed up in one word. Spirit.

When we talk about spirit, we do not need to interfere with any religious or philosophical beliefs. The spirit that we are talking about is more basic and organic than that. It is the kind of spirit that inspires kindness toward others, art, and enjoyment of life, among many other positive things in this world.

In this respect, tai chi transcends its aspects of martial arts, healing, and philosophy and sees them for what they are: building blocks along a path. But the path is infinite. I recently heard a philosopher on the radio who was trying to define what it is that makes humans different from other animals. The conclusion that he came to was that humans are different because they try to be more than human. This could be through technology, art, or any other medium.

I liked the definition because in a way it encapsulates tai chi. By refining our spirit, we are striving to be something that is in some way an improvement on what we already are.

The way of tai chi, then, is a way of self-improvement through the spirit. The key to unlocking the spirit is to play it from the heart and to practice because you really love it and have a passion for it.

Index

Credits and Acknowledgements

With the greatest of thanks to my teachers, Christopher Pei, of the U.S. Wushu Academy; Shelagh Grandpierre, of the Tai Chi Alliance; Sue Hix and Tom Litten, of the Rosewell Shiatsu Centre in Lincolnshire; Peter Warr, of Wu Kung U.K.; and Mike Webster, of Waveform Energetics. And, of course, to my wife, Carol, for her enduring patience!

  The author and publishers would like to thank our models, Caron Bosler, Channing Bosler, Graham Dalton, and Venetia Tuckey.

Bibliography

Reid, Howard. *Soft Martial Arts*.
Su Lu Tang. *Xing Y: Quan Yue—The Study of Form Mind Boxing*.
Wile, Douglas. *Yang Family Secret Transmissions*.
Wilheim, Richard (translator). *I-Ching*.
Yu Shenquan. *Chen-style Taijiquan*.

Picture Credits

Pp. 6, 42 © Corbis; pp. 10, 20, 22–23, 25–27, 28–29, 31, 35, 36–37 © Stockbyte; pp. 16, 27, 35 © Getty Images.